JOY

JOY

Bertrand Weaver, C. P.

SHEED AND WARD – *New York*

Library of Congress Catalog Card Number: 64-19912

Cum Permissu Superiorum
Gerard Rooney, C.P.
Provincial

Nihil Obstat:
James T. Clarke, S.T.L.
Censor Librorum
May 19, 1964

Imprimatur:
✠ *Jerome D. Hannan*
Bishop of Scranton
May 22, 1964

Manufactured in the United States of America

To the Virgin of Guadalupe
Joy of the Americas
Called by Pius XI
Queen of All the Americas
Hailed by Pius XII
Empress of America
Invoked by John XXIII
Mother and Mistress
of
The Peoples of America
Celestial Missionary of the New World

Foreword

Ours is a joyless age, if its literature reports it truly, a time of rootlessness and uncertainty. Yet our era is by no means joyless for all, despite the prevailing mood. There are many people, under the same stress and shadows as their gloom-struck fellows, who possess their souls in peace and make joyful melody in their hearts. They are not fools or fatalists. Rather, they are profoundly Christian.

Faith, hope and love irradiate all reality for them, and their own life and lot in particular. In spite of adverse circumstances, they are secure and serene in their identity as children of God, brothers and co-heirs with Christ. They enter into the Savior's sacrifice as re-presented at the altar, are nourished by his body and blood, and see their sorrows and sufferings as a privileged share in his cross, keep ever in mind that heaven is their destination. Hence their joy, lively and imperishable.

The secret of that joy is set forth by Father Weaver in the pages which follow. He has searched it to the roots and explains it lucidly. He makes it concrete and wonderfully attractive. The reader is kindled with joy as he attends to Father Weaver, and will be lighted and warmed by it long after he has put aside this quickening book.

MSGR. JOHN S. KENNEDY

Contents

JOY

Introduction

Few things have harmed religion more than the impression that its practice leads to sadness. It requires only a glance at the saints to realize that the opposite is true. They manifest the vibrant joy of belief, while the proponents of unbelief often present a picture of withering gloom.

Oscar Wilde, who experienced the peace and joy of Catholicism only on his deathbed in Paris, in the days of his disbelief wrote with a sadness that you can almost taste, touch and smell: "When I think of religion at all, I feel as if I would like to found an order for those who cannot believe; the Confraternity of all the Fatherless one might call it, where on an altar on which no taper burned, a priest, in whose heart peace had no dwelling, might celebrate with unblessed bread and a chalice empty of wine." To which St. Philip Neri would have replied: "Christian joy is a gift of God, flowing from a good conscience."

A Fueurbach says that the world is a madhouse, a jail, and a St. Thomas Aquinas says that happiness is the natural life of man. A Schopenhauer observes that life is a sham, an annoying and useless interruption of the steady calm of eternal nothingness, and a St. John of the Cross says that the soul of one who serves God always swims in joy, always keeps holiday, and is always in the mood for singing. A Swinburne opines that earthly existence is "filled with days we would not fain behold, and nights we would not hear of," and a St. John Vianney holds that it is always springtime in the heart that loves God.

St. Teresa of Avila, who founded so many convents of contemplative nuns and is recognized as a genius even outside the Church, said that she feared nothing so much as seeing her spiritual daughters lose their joy of soul. She held that not joy but joylessness is the mother of dissipation. The cheerfulness of priests, monks and nuns is proverbial. St. Francis of Assisi, and his disciple, St. Anthony of Padua, both sang on their deathbeds. It is significant that the unsaintly Franciscan, Brother Elias, regarded it as unseemly for St. Francis to do so.

It was said of St. Romuald that just to see him made people glad. St. Dominic gave such an impression of joyousness that men, women and children ran after him as he walked. Erasmus observed of St. Thomas More that he was one of the happiest men he had ever met. It is remarked of St. Vincent de Paul that those who met him were made joyful by the gladness that shone in his face.

Barbara Ward wrote that going from the antiseptic environment in which the children of Northern Europe are raised to the tumbling, pulsating atmosphere in which the children of Italy grow up is like going from a well-kept sanitarium to a lively, merry playground. It was another British Catholic, Hilaire Belloc, noted for his joyful bounce, who wrote:

> But Catholic men that live upon wine
> Are deep in the water, and frank, and fine;
> Wherever I travel I find it so,
> *Benedicamus Domino.*[1]

[1] Hilaire Belloc, "Heretics All" in *Sonnets and Verse* (New York, Sheed and Ward, 1944).

Joy, as considered in this book, is far from the artificial gaiety implied in the tired suggestion: *Keep smiling.* A smile induced in this way is more likely to be a grimace. Joy of soul is not something that you turn on, as you would turn on a light. It is not something that is to be sought directly. It is a by-product of the doctrines and practices of the Faith. Joy is an overflow. It overflows from the Christian life, when that life is lived fully.

It is not a joy that can be measured, as is true, more or less, of sensible joy. In connection with the latter, a person will say that he enjoyed himself on a particular occasion. He will say that he enjoyed the day, or the evening, or the trip, or the vacation. We can measure, in a way, the satisfaction that we have received in the physical or intellectual order. But the current of serene joy that flows in our spirits cannot be charted.

There are occasions, it is true, when spiritual joy leaps within us. Any priest can tell of times when he has received a convert, or has received back a prodigal son or daughter, and has observed joy well up in the soul of the person who has experienced a new communion with God. But most of the time, spiritual joy is an undercurrent. It flows along quietly, giving us a general sense of tranquility. It is not incompatible with deep grief or great trial.

Perhaps the best illustration of the mingling of this joy with the sorrows and troubles of earthly life is the Gulf Stream. This famous current of warm water, which flows from the Gulf of Mexico along the Eastern coast of North America, is separated from the coast by a narrow strip of cold water. The hardships of life may be compared with the cold-water strip that lies alongside the Gulf Stream. As the Gulf Stream proceeds on its way north, it tends to drag other water along with it. As more water becomes involved, its speed decreases and its boundaries become indefinite. In a similar way, the cold facts and events of life may prevent us from feeling sensibly the warmth of spiritual joy for long or short periods, but they cannot essentially affect that deep current of joy which is an effect of the presence of the Holy Spirit within us.

Ordinarily, the key word in the title of a book of this kind would be *happiness.* I have chosen to stress *joy* because, for one reason, happiness is an overworked word. Another is that joy goes beyond happiness, being a complement of the latter. St. Thomas explains that the very seeing of God, which is an act of the intellect, is substantially and fundamentally our happiness. He goes on to add that the seeing of God with our intellect is followed by supreme joy. This joy belongs to the will and is a formal complement of happiness. Thus he concludes that the ultimate basis of happiness is in the vision; its complement is in the fruition.

Dante evidently was commenting on this idea of St. Thomas when he wrote:

> You must know that all have delight
> in so far as their sight penetrates
> into truth which quiets doubt.
> Hence one can see how happiness
> is found in the act of beholding
> not on that of loving, which follows later.

1. The Joy of Faith

The word *thing* is without doubt one of the most useful of all words. One does not, however, expect it to be used of something of overwhelming importance. It is used ordinarily of subjects or objects which are unimportant: "What is that *thing?*" someone will ask. Or it is used in pity or contempt in reference to some person who has been reduced to a particularly unhappy or miserable state: "the poor *thing.*" On the other hand, this word can suddenly be used of matters of vital importance. If one were caught in a blizzard in an automobile with the engine gone dead, one would naturally say: "The *thing* is to get the motor running."

Even though *thing* may represent a matter of great importance, we are still surprised that it should be used in reference to something sublime. Yet, writers like G. K. Chesterton and Joyce Kilmer used it effectively in connection with the Catholic Faith. Chesterton, whose intellect probed the universe and winged above it, decided that the most fitting title for the story of his conversion was: "The *Thing:* Why I am a Catholic." Kilmer made use of *thing* in an identical sense when he wrote that the Catholic Faith was such a *thing* that he would rather write moderately well about it than magnificently well about anything else.

These men were saying what every sincere convert to the

Catholic Faith has thought and felt on his entrance into the Church: "This is the *thing* I have been looking for to satisfy my mind and heart." When a person has found the *one thing* in the whole world which is the key to everything else, the joy resulting from this discovery is bound to be unique. When an outstanding American woman gave the reasons for her conversion in a lengthy magazine article, she was criticized for writing about it so soon after the event. Her reply could not have been more to the point. She simply said that when you have heard good news, you want to tell it.

The fundamental reason for joy in the Faith is that faith opens up a whole new and wonderful world. We have a way of thinking and speaking about *the other world* as though we were going to enter it only when we die. The fact is that we are living in the other world now. The other world is not only all about us but *within* us. The joy of the convert is the joy of discovery of this new and exciting and infinite world. If the joy of a born Catholic in some cases does not equal that of a convert, it is because the former has allowed his faith to become dulled.

Only if the unseen God and the invisible realities of the other world become as real to us as the things we see and hear and touch and taste and smell can we experience the true joy of faith. We talk about *the other world,* but this is a small phrase to use for such an infinite reality. People become excited when there is talk of adventures in outer space and interplanetary travel, but all this has to do with the finite universe. Vast as the universe is, it is paltry when compared with the unseen, infinite world of the spirit.

Hebrews uses *thing* in the sublime way we referred to above in its description of faith. We read that faith "convinces us of *things* we cannot see" (Heb. 11:1).[1] The degree of our joy in the Faith depends on the degree in which we grasp these tremendous unseen *things.* In the Acts of the Apostles we read that God "had opened to the Gentiles a door of faith" (14:26, CV).[2] Faith is the doorway to the unseen world. It is obvious that everybody who enters that doorway believes. It is also evident that all do not believe in the same degree. As one who enters the doorway of some majestic cathedral can stand just over the threshold, or go part way up the nave, or go all the way and enter the sanctuary, so it is with passing over the threshold of faith and entering the unseen world.

Those whose faith is weak, who just about step over the threshold, have a rather dim view of the things of the invisible world. Those whose faith is middling, have a middling view of the realities of the unseen world. Those whose faith is strong, who briskly step over the threshold and penetrate as far as possible into the other world, have a splendid view of its realities.

Joy results from the possession of one's desires. We possess God (or are possessed by him) through hope and love, but hope and love cannot exist unless faith precedes them. We begin our approach to God through faith. Those who have a strong faith know the joy that the psalmist felt when he sang: "Thou art near, O Lord." St. Paul expresses this idea in another way when he writes that through faith we have "confident access." He means confident

[1] Unless otherwise indicated, the scriptural quotations in this book are from *The Holy Bible,* trans. Ronald Knox. Copyright 1944, 1948 and 1950, Sheed and Ward, Inc. Reprinted with the permission of His Eminence, the Cardinal Archbishop of Westminster.

[2] *The Holy Bible,* Confraternity Edition. Copyright 1953, 1962, The Confraternity of Christian Doctrine. Reprinted with the permission of His Eminence, the Cardinal Archbishop of Westminster.

access to the invisible God. If those who have easy access to a temporal superior are considered fortunate, far more happy are those who, through the possession of faith, have easy access to the God of the visible and invisible worlds.

When St. Paul came upon an altar at Athens with the inscription "To the Unknown God," he used it as a springboard for a discourse to the men of the city who had gathered in the place, which must have been similar to Hyde Park in London or Union Square in New York. He told his listeners that it had been determined from the beginning that men "should seek God, and perhaps grope after him and find him, *though he is not far from any one of us.* For in him we live and move and have our being." (Acts 17:27-28, CV) He was referring to God's presence in all creation. This is called his omnipresence. But he is present in a far different and more wonderful way to those who have faith.

Recounting the confidence with which Moses led the Hebrews out of Egypt, Scripture says that the patriarch acted "as if seeing him who cannot be seen" (Heb. 11:27, CV). We can visualize Moses leaving the land of bondage, with that mass of people following, as though he could see God walking at his side. The joy that sprang from his faith must have caused him to walk with giant strides, with a song in his heart and on his lips.

Abraham, a man of such prodigious faith that he is called by St. Paul the father of all believers, had a joy in walking and talking with God that we can sense strongly after four thousand years. Christ showed the Jews that this joy was increased by the fact that his faith enabled Abraham to peer through two thousand years and behold our Lord as the Messias: "Abraham your father rejoiced that he was to see my day. He saw it and was glad." (Jn. 8:56, CV)

Another striking example of the joy of being close to God through faith is found in Jacob. After his dream about the ladder on which he saw angels ascending and descending, Scripture says that he was trembling. We may readily believe that he was trembling with joy, as is indicated by his words: "How awesome is this place! This is none other than the house of God; this is the gate of heaven!" (Gen. 28:17, CV) And after he had wrestled with the angel and obtained his blessing, his joy was full as he declared: "I have seen God face to face!" (Gen. 32:30). Of course, he had not really seen God, and he had seen an angel only in human form. But, like Moses, he was filled with joy, "as if seeing him who cannot be seen" (Heb. 11:27, CV).

It was the deep and vivid faith of the founder of the Passionists, St. Paul of the Cross, which caused him to enjoy on earth such a consciousness of God that he could say without exaggeration that he could not understand how anybody could be found who was not always thinking of God. His contemporary, St. Vincent Strambi, Passionist bishop, wrote that St. Paul of the Cross "talked with such certainty, vivacity and reality about the things of the other world that he appeared to see them with his bodily eyes." Here we have the joy of proximity to the object of one's desires. St. Paul was so close to the unseen world that he could talk about the realities of that world with the same sureness that he might manifest in speaking about some tree in the monastery garden.

While it is true that the massive "door of faith" has been swung open for us by God, giving us entrance to the unseen world, he expects us to penetrate, by our own effort, the many doorways of that world. We should not expect God to carry us over the various thresholds. There is some walking to be done by us if we are going to explore, discover and enjoy what lies hidden from our physical sight.

God has given us faith, but whether this faith is going to be practical, whether it is going to affect our day-to-day lives, depends to a great extent on our willingness to work at applying it. We talk about *exercising our faith,* and exercising requires effort in the spiritual order as well as in the physical. As da Vinci said: "Thou, O Lord, dost give us all good things at the price of labor."

Faith makes us realize, for instance, that we are always in the presence of God, that his eye is upon us unceasingly. But because it is all too easy to forget his presence, we often have to exercise our faith by making a conscious effort to remember that he is standing by. It takes a lot of practice of one's faith in God's presence to become convinced, as St. Paul of the Cross was, that God is closer to us than our skin is to our flesh.

Only if we remember God's presence will we have the joy of acting as though seeing him who cannot be seen. It does not require much discernment to understand how much more joy there would be in our lives, and in our homes, factories and offices, if those who believe were to exercise their belief that God is present amid the activity of the home, the noise of the factory, the bustle of the office.

Another practical aspect of our faith is the degree of our consciousness of the reality of Christ. All this joy in believing is, after all, bound up with belief in Christ. He is the doorway to the other world, to the unseen God. "I am the door," he said (Jn. 10:9, CV). He is the door because he has opened his person as God and man to let us through to the Godhead. He has thus lessened the distance between God and man, but unless a living faith makes us conscious of Christ's life within us, we will only increase the distance between God and ourselves.

St. Paul was writing to those who already believed in Christ when he said: "May Christ find a dwelling-place, through faith, in your hearts" (Eph. 3:17). Such an indwelling of Christ, through faith, is only the beginning of a life of faith. St. Paul wanted all believers to have such a living and practical faith that they could say with him: "For me, life means Christ" (Phil. 1:21). If we who believe in Christ have an active faith, we will not keep him locked up in our hearts. Those around us will have the joy of seeing Christ in our actions. The joy of Christ will be reflected and refracted in a thousand encouraging words, friendly gestures, unselfish acts of generosity.

When our belief in Christ is a living, pulsating thing, we experience the throbbing joy with which Patrick hymned Christ:

> Christ, as a light, illumine and guide me!
> Christ, as a shield, o'ershadow and cover me!
> Christ, be under me! Christ, be over me!
> Christ, be beside me, on left hand and right!
> Christ, be before me, behind me, about me!
> Christ, this day, be within and without me!
> Christ, the lowly and meek,
> Christ, the all-powerful,
> Be in the heart of each to whom I speak,
> In the mouth of each who speaks to me,
> In all who draw near me,
> Or see me, or hear me!

We believe that Christ is either in the heart of every person we meet and deal with, or that he can find his way there. We can, in a sense, pray Christ into the heart of every person with whom we begin to talk. If our faith is strong, it will persuade us that we can bring the life of Christ, and the joy of it, not only to those with whom we live and work, but to those who are fellow-passengers on a train, bus, or plane.

The way in which we exercise our faith also determines how vividly we see the tremendous spiritual realities which lie behind the visible ceremonies of the liturgy. With a little effort, the silent, stolid, remote attitude that characterizes so many who assist at Mass could be replaced by one of joyful participation in the eucharistic mystery. By the exercise of their faith, they could cause the scales to fall from their spiritual sight. They would then look up at the altar and have the joy of seeing not only Christ's visible minister, but the great High Priest himself changing the bread and wine into his body and blood, and offering himself in sacrifice as he did on the Cross on the first Good Friday.

Only those who, by the exercise of their faith, look beyond visible realities to those that are invisible can have the joy of seeing:

> Christ of the supper room,
> Christ of the empty tomb,
> Christ of the Day of Doom
> in this White Host.[3]

When we fail to exercise our faith, we leave unsaid ten thousand prayers that could find their way to the heart of God. Since we believe that God hears and heeds our slight-

[3] Robert Farren, "Immolation" in *Thronging Feet* (New York, Sheed and Ward, 1936).

est aspiration, it is supremely foolish to forego the joy of answered prayer by not being attuned to the unseen world through a vibrant faith.

Everything that is good in our lives is rooted in our faith. St. Paul wrote to the young bishop Timothy about "*thriving* on the principles of that faith whose wholesome doctrine thou hast followed" (I Tim. 4:6). Whether we have the joy of thriving spiritually depends on how strongly we are rooted in faith. Whether justice thrives in us by giving God and man what is their due, whether we practice prudence by arranging our lives wisely, whether we show the fortitude of sons of God and brothers of Christ, whether we are temperate in the use of God's gifts, all these things depend on how deeply we are rooted in faith. It was the realization of this which prompted Gerard Manley Hopkins' prayer to the "Giver of breath and bread," "send my roots rain."

The prophet Habacuc described what it means to be a *true believer* when he said: "by his faith he lives, who lives right" (2:4). St. Paul was paraphrasing the prophet when he wrote: "It is faith that brings life to the just man" (Rom. 1:17). We become believers through the act of faith. We have the joy of *true believers* when the act of faith leads to a life that is alive with faith, a life that is permeated by a spirit of faith. So convinced of all this were the Apostles that they blurted out: "Lord, give us more faith" (Lk. 17:5).

Even during our earthly life, we can say that one door in the invisible world leads to another. There is even now the joy of going from unseen reality to unseen reality. Discovery follows discovery in the infinite, invisible world of the spirit. St. Peter was talking about our joy in Christ in this life when he said with exuberance: "In him, though you do not see him, yet believing, you exult with a joy unspeakable and triumphant" (I Pet. 1:8, CV).

While we look forward to the joy that will flood our souls in the life of the world to come, let us not play down the joy that we now have in believing. The joy that is ours now in believing is the seed that contains our eternal joy, just as the faith that is ours now is the seed that contains the glorious light in which we shall see God in heaven.

2. *The Joy of Hope*

Just as many fail to understand the place that the Third Person of the Holy Trinity has in our lives, so they are slow in seeing the importance of hope in the trinity of theological virtues. Because we neglect the virtue of hope, we deprive ourselves of the deep joy that the exercise of this virtue is calculated to bring us. The three theological virtues of faith, hope and charity are absolutely necessary for reaching eternal life. We are conscious of the need for faith and love, but we do not seem to recognize our need for hope.

Through faith we *see,* as it were, the invisible God and the realities of the unseen world. Through hope we begin to *embrace* God and the things of God. Faith brings satisfaction to our minds, and hope brings satisfaction to our hearts. What is seen by the mind may leave us cold. It is only when we possess what we see that we are really satisfied.

In the chapter on joy in faith, the famous definition of that virtue in Hebrews was quoted. Rather, that part of the definition was given where it says that faith is the evidence of things unseen. The first part of the definition links faith with hope. It says that faith *"is that which gives substance to our hopes"* (Heb. 11:1). Scripture is emphasizing that faith is only the first step toward God, a passing over the threshold of the unseen world. We start to share in the riches of that world through hope.

Hope is to faith what the fruit is to the blossom. If we did not go from faith to hope, our very faith would be stunted. Cherry and apple blossoms are beautiful, but we would feel cheated if their short life did not fulfill its promise by the later appearance of the fruit. St. Paul shows hope to be the fructification of faith when he says: "May God, the author of our hope, fill you with all joy and peace in your believing; so that you may have hope in abundance, through the power of the Holy Spirit" (Rom. 15:13).

A brief consideration of the definition of the virtue of hope will convince us of the reasons we have for exulting in the possession of such a virtue. It is the supernatural, theological virtue which inclines us to expect with firm confidence eternal life and the means to reach it. We have this firm confidence because our hope is based on the infinite power, mercy and fidelity of God, to whom we are not just creatures but sons and daughters.

Christ reminded the Jews that, while they took care of their sons' wants with paternal solicitude, their interest in providing for their children was a pale reflection of the solicitude and generosity that God bestows on those who trust in him. Here we are dealing with a Father who is infinitely powerful, rich, merciful and loving. Our joy is in the realization that all this power, wealth, mercy and love are waiting to be released through our practice of the virtue of hope.

Our joy is rendered more secure because there is not in supernatural hope the kind of insecurity that is often an element in natural hope. A person could hope, for instance, to come into a fortune, but his hope would be made uncertain by the fact that there is many a slip between the cup and the lip. The slip could take the form of plotting relatives, death, or any of a number of other factors. And should the individual acquire the fortune, there would loom other factors that might snatch it from him, or prevent his enjoyment of it.

The two main objects of our spiritual hope are grace here and glory hereafter. Both these objects have joyful aspects. When we refer to grace, we have in mind both sanctifying and actual grace. If we are to preserve sanctifying grace, on the possession of which at death our eternal happiness depends, we need an unending chain of actual graces. It is obviously a source of joy to realize that God is going to keep these graces flowing as long as we hope for them. Holy Scripture calls this chain of graces "the anchorage of our souls." We read in the Epistle to the Hebrews: "Two irrevocable assurances, over which there could be no question of God deceiving us, were to bring firm confidence to us poor castaways, bidding us cling to the hope we have in view, the anchorage of our souls. Sure and immovable, it reaches that inner sanctuary beyond the veil, which Jesus Christ, our escort, has entered already, a high priest, now, eternally, with the priesthood of Melchisedech." (6:18-20)

If we want to experience the full joy of hope, our hope must reach the stage where it almost becomes a new virtue, that of trust. Trust in God is an intensification of the virtue of hope. St. Thomas says that "trust means primarily that hope which a man conceives when he relies on the word of someone whose help has been promised him." One of life's greatest joys is to have friends whom we can trust absolutely, trust with every last material possession, trust with our personal problems, trust with the secrets of our hearts. We might hesitate to use the word friendship to describe the relationship between God and man had not Christ used this expression when he said to the Apostles at the Last Supper: "and so I have called you my friends" (Jn. 15:15). If friendship has one essential quality, it is trust.

It is said of Abraham that he "put his faith in God, and it was reckoned virtue in him, and he earned the title of God's friend" (Jas. 2:23). The faith referred to in this quotation is not so much faith in the sense of believing. It is more the virtue of trust. It was also Moses' absolute trust that made him worthy of God's friendship. The Book of Exodus says that "the Lord spoke with Moses, face to face, as a man speaks to his friend" (33:11).

Very likely the most powerful recorded expression of trust in God is the cry of Job: "Although he should kill me, I will trust in him" (13:15, CV). This happened when his friends taunted him over his indescribable misfortunes. These included the sudden death of all his children, the loss of his innumerable cattle and sheep and of his own health; he was stricken with an ulcerous sore, "from head to foot, so that he was fain to sit him down on the dunghill, and scratch himself with a shard where he itched" (2:8).

We think of faith as the outstanding virtue of Abraham, the father of all believers. But it would be impossible to find a better example of faith subtly blending into hope and trust. When God told Abraham that he would beget a son in his extreme old age, St. Paul says that he trusted God to keep his promise, not doubting even though "he was nearly a hundred years old at the time," or even because of "the deadness of Sara's womb" (Rom. 4:19). If we trust in God, the physically impossible will not affect our acceptance of his word. He will work miracles, if necessary, for those who trust in him. The promise of a son at their advanced age was so fantastic that Sara laughed when she heard it. But Scripture says that "Abraham, then, believed, hoping against hope; and thus became the father of many nations" (Rom. 4:19). All this trust on the part of Abraham was rewarded by his ecstatic joy when he took into his arms the son for whom he had waited almost a hundred years.

Abraham's long wait for the fulfillment of his hope of having a son illustrates why the joy of our hope is not a present, pulsating thing. The complete fulfillment of our hope will not be experienced until the vision of God breaks upon us and floods our being with a joy of which we get only hints in this world. As a result of this waiting, one of the elements in our hope must be patience. St. Paul explains this when he writes that we are "waiting for that adoption which is the ransoming of our bodies from their slavery. It must be so, since our salvation is founded upon the hope of something. Hope would not be hope at all if its object were in view; how could a man still hope for something which he sees? And if we are hoping for something still unseen, then we need endurance to wait for it." (Rom. 8:23)

Another striking example of a hope that was willing to wait for joyous fulfillment was that of Moses. The daughter of Pharao offered to pass him off as her son. Scripture says: "He preferred ill-usage, shared with the people of God, to the brief enjoyment of sinful pleasures; all the wealth of Egypt could not so enrich him as the despised lot of God's anointed; he had eyes, you see, for nothing but the promised reward" (Heb. 11:25-26).

Whether we take the short view of hope, as the virtue which causes us to expect year by year, month by month, week by week, day by day, hour by hour, the present necessary actual graces to overcome temptation or to practice virtue, or the long view, which causes us to expect eternal life, the substratum of joy accompanying hope may appear almost nonexistent. If a person is bowed under a rain of hard knocks—disappointment, illness, disloyalty of friends, financial reverses, family trouble, misunderstanding—it is going to be difficult to see an omnipotent and loving Father waiting to reach out a helping hand in time of trial, much less to give joy in such a time. And yet, for one who believes and trusts, there is joy in recalling the words of the psalmist, who was without many of the supports that we have: "Wait patiently for the Lord to help thee; be brave, and let thy heart take comfort; wait patiently for the Lord" (26:13). There is even more joy in remembering the words of our Lord: "Are not sparrows sold two for a penny? And yet it is impossible for one of them to fall to the ground without your heavenly Father's will. And as for you, he takes every hair of your head into his reckoning." (Matt. 10:29-30)

We grasp the full import of the virtue of hope only if we understand the counterpoint between God's strength and our weakness. God made this contrast clear to St. Paul after the Apostle had asked three times for the removal of what he described obscurely as "a sting to distress my outward nature, an angel of Satan to rebuff me." To St.

Paul's plea God replied: "My grace is enough for thee; my strength finds its full scope in thy weakness." After this moving confession of weakness and strength, the weakness being his own, the strength from God, he shows his joy in placing all his hope and confidence in the Lord: "More than ever, then, I delight to boast of the weaknesses that humiliate me, so that the strength of Christ may enshrine itself in me." (II Cor. 12:7-10)

In our own time, a cloistered nun who lived to be only twenty-four, by her limitless trust has opened new horizons of hope. Learned theologians have written one study after another, analyzing the doctrine of St. Therese of the Child Jesus. She would have smiled at all this probing by scholars of what she called her "little way." It is not an oversimplification to say that her doctrine is summed up in her statement that we can never have too much confidence in our God, who is so mighty and so merciful, for according to the measure of our hope in him, we shall receive.

If there has been a particular saint to whom God could say, "My strength finds its full scope in thy weakness," it is this exemplar of the virtue of trust. Most of us are inclined to hope and trust *in spite of* our weakness. St. Therese trusted *on account of* it. She wrote: "We live in an age of inventions; nowadays there are elevators to spare us the trouble of climbing stairs. I will try to find an elevator to raise me to God, for I am too small to climb the steep stairway of perfection." The "elevator" was a trust in God so complete that it has been universally called her *doctrine of abandonment.* This abandonment is such a distinctive characteristic in her life that one would almost suppose that she had invented it. Hers was the joy of expecting everything from God the way a little child expects everything from his father.

The joy of her hope vibrates in her breathless declaration: "Even now I know it! Yes, all my hopes will be fulfilled. Truly the Lord will do wonders for me, infinitely surpassing my boundless desires." It is doubtful whether any member of the Church has manifested greater hope than that reflected in St. Therese's superbly confident prediction: "After my death, I shall let fall a shower of roses." One cannot imagine greater trust than that.

While we rejoice because our hope gives us assurance of God's unfailing support during our earthly life, we should imitate St. Therese in not losing sight of that eternal glory which is the main object of our hope. When we are tempted to think that the eternal bliss which we are ultimately working for is very far away, we should think of that hope which is in all of us, and which prompted the author of the Epistle to the Hebrews to write: "Only a brief moment, now, before he who is coming will be here; he will not linger on the way" (10:37). A mistake evidently made by many is to allow their hope of heaven to weaken. In a sort of desperate fashion, they seem satisfied if their passage over the sea of earthly life is not too rough and hazardous. They do not give much thought to reaching port. This is to have the virtue of hope lie dormant. Such a hope is like a bud that fails to unfold and reveal the flower of which it is the promise.

Of the word of God, on which our hope rests, Scripture says: ". . . it will go on shining, like a lamp in some darkened room, until the dawn breaks, and the day-star rises in your hearts" (II Pet. 1:19). And St. Paul reminds us that we are "to look forward, blessed in our hope, to the day when there will be a new dawn of glory, the glory of the great God, the glory of our Savior Jesus Christ" (Titus 2:13). Through the Savior was fulfilled what David had sung many years before: "For all those who trust in thee there is joy and everlasting triumph" (Ps. 5:12).

3. *The Joy of Love of God*

What is most important to a Christian at any given moment of his earthly life is whether he is in the state of grace or in a state of mortal sin. Unless his conscience is dead or benumbed, a person of faith who is in mortal sin is bound to be miserable. On the other hand, a person who feels he is in the state of grace can maintain a spirit of joy even though enduring great vexations.

Falling into a state of mortal sin, and thus out of the state of grace, is simply falling away from God and his love. It means losing the third of the theological virtues, which is charity, or love of God. It is the break-up of the most important of all friendships, that between God and man.

A man who retains faith and hope, but in whom love of God has died, believes in the unseen God, in whom formerly he had such delight, and clings precariously to God and the things of God through hope, but he realizes that now he and his God are at enmity. The thought that he is separated from him for whom he was made, and for whom he has an insatiable hunger, fills his mouth with the taste of ashes.

Not all the lovers of God have been able to give utterance to their longing for him with the same power of expression. A man with David's ecstatic delight in God is not born every year. His joy in God was expressed in such poetic outbursts as: "O God, my whole soul longs for thee, as a deer for running water; my whole soul thirsts for God, the living God" (Ps. 41:2-3).

St. Augustine, who had tried earthly loves, reached the stage where the love of God was the one love that really mattered. With matchless wisdom and beauty, he expresses his rapture: "Yet in a sense I do love light and melody and fragrance and food and embrace when I love my God—the light and the voice and the fragrance and the food and embrace in the soul, when that light shines upon my soul which no place can contain, that voice sounds which no time can take from me, I breathe that fragrance which no wind scatters, I eat the food which is not lessened by eating, and I lie in the embrace which satiety never comes to sunder. This is that I love, when I love my God."[1]

It is hardly surprising that there are so many parts of Holy Scripture which leap and dance with joy, for this is the book which tells the story of God's friendship with man. "Clap your hands, all you nations, in applause, acclaim your God with cries of rejoicing," sings the psalmist exultantly . . . "the Lord goes up, loudly the trumpets peal. A psalm, a psalm for our God, a psalm, a psalm for our King! God is King of all the earth; sound the hymn of praise." (46:2-8) And Jeremias says: ". . . you shall hear cries of joy and mirth, voice of bridegroom and voice of

[1] *The Confessions of St. Augustine,* trans. by F. J. Sheed (New York, Sheed and Ward, 1943), Bk. X, ch. 6.

bride. There you shall hear men singing, Give thanks to the Lord, the Lord is gracious, his mercy endures forever. . . ." (33:11)

Those who have tasted the joy of God's love find nothing in the world so depressing as the tawdry illicit human loves which men and women use as substitutes for the one love which alone can satisfy the human heart. True human love is a thing of beauty and joy, but the most perfect human being could never bring fulfillment to a soul that was made for union with the God who not only created it, but died for it. The Devil leads people a cruel and futile chase. It is like watching mice in a maze, running, running, only to come up ceaselessly against blind walls and dead ends.

Francis Thompson was referring to the love of God when he wrote that *"love is a many-splendored thing."* One cannot fail to be struck with the tragedy of human beings falling in love with reflections of God's beauty, power, goodness and intelligence in their fellow-creatures, when God, the source of all that is attractive in creatures, goes unloved. But his goodness will not allow them to be satisfied with mere reflections of himself. He makes them feel dissatisfaction with purely earthly loves. It is this dissatisfaction which explains why most love songs are songs of lament, songs of disappointed love. Love is meant to be a thing of singing joy, but when it is sought exclusively in illusory—or even in real—reflections of God, instead of in God himself, it finds fitting expression in singing the blues.

Plato had a wise pagan's insight into this when he wrote: "Now he who has been corrupted does not easily rise out of this world to the sight of true beauty in the other; he looks only at her earthly namesake, and instead of being awed by the sight of her, he is given over to pleasure, and like a brutish beast, he rushes to enjoy and beget; he consorts with wantonness, and is not afraid or ashamed of pursuing pleasure in violation of nature."

If we are going to have an authentic joy in our love of God, the love itself has to be authentic. This brings us to a consideration of what this love is. There are some false ideas about it which we must be prepared to reject before we can understand its true meaning. It is not a sentimental thing; this would be unworthy of the majesty of God. It is not an emotional love, although emotion may at times accompany it. It does not consist in words, for it is possible that a person who often has the words *O God, I love thee* on his lips has not much of this love in his heart.

To love God is nothing else than to have one's will united with his will. This means wanting to see God's will exalted and fulfilled by all those of his creatures who possess free will. The sincerity of our love of God is determined by the way in which we personally go about the work of carrying out his will. If we say we want his will accomplished by mankind, but fail to start fulfilling it ourselves, our love is clearly hollow and hypocritical.

We have noted that an essential element in friendship is trust. But it would be a strange sort of friendship in which the friends merely trusted one another. Along with trust, friends expect affection from each other. Our friendship with God begins with faith and hope, but it is not complete until it develops into love. One of the proofs that love is present in a friendship is the mutual concern that friends have for each other's interest. The only way we can show we are concerned about God's interest is through zeal that his will be done. Our Lord summed it all up when he said to the Apostles: "And you, if you do all that I command you, are my friends" (Jn. 15:14).

God manifests his will in two chief ways: through his commandments and through the events of life. In another chapter, we will consider the latter manifestation of his will, that is, the circumstances, happy and unhappy, in which we find ourselves during our pilgrimage to eternity. Here we are more concerned about the proof of our love of God through obedience to his law.

If we want to rejoice in the love of God, we must rejoice in his commandments, for God has made love of him and obedience to him two sides of the one coin. Christ could not have stated this more clearly and succinctly than he did when he said: "The man who loves me is the man who keeps the commandments he has from me" (Jn. 14:21). And St. John seems to identify the love of God with obeying his law when he says: "Loving God means keeping his commandments." And immediately, as though to say that love makes keeping them a joy, he adds: "And these commandments of his are not a burden to us." (I Jn. 5:3)

Joy in God's commandments is nowhere better reflected than in the 118th Psalm: "Blithely as one that has found great possessions, I follow thy decrees. . . . Be thy covenant ever my delight. . . . Each command of thine I embrace lovingly. . . . Flung wide my arms to greet thy law, ever in my thoughts thy bidding. . . . Precious beyond gold or jewel I hold thy law." (14, 16, 40, 48, 127)

The perfection of love of God, which results in perfect joy in God, is reached only when our wills are perfectly attuned to his, only when we want him exalted, honored and glorified, only when we personally are intent on doing everything we do for his greater glory. Only then can we say with utter sincerity the words of the Gloria of the Mass, *We give thee thanks for thy great glory.* Only when we rejoice that God is God can we taste the full joy of loving God.

Anything that is true, good or beautiful in a creature is only a reflection of the God of truth, goodness and beauty. God must, when he sees his infinite perfection, love himself. He must also love any reflection of his own perfection. Seeing such a reflection of himself in us, he loves us.

Genesis says that God declared in the beginning: "Let us make man, wearing our own image and likeness" (1:26). All men are in the image of God, because all have an intellect and a will which resemble the intelligence and will of God. But men begin to grow like God only when they embrace truth with their intellects and goodness with their wills. God must love his image in all human beings, but he can be united in love only with those who are like him through the possession of truth and goodness. "If a man has any love for me, he will be true to my word; and then he will win my Father's love, and we will both come to him, and make our continual abode with him" (Jn. 14:23). Since our search for truth and goodness leads us more deeply into the embrace of the God of truth and goodness, there is joy in the very search.

Pygmalion, a king of Cyprus, made an ivory statue of a maiden and put so much of his own concept of beauty into it that he fell in love with it. According to mythology, the goddess of love and beauty, at his prayer, brought the statue to life. A number of artistic works have sprung from this Greek myth. The most recent popular success was the musical comedy made from George Bernard Shaw's play, in which a professor changed a cockney hoyden into a cultured lady. That audiences found unusual satisfaction in it was evident from its record run.

It was so well received because those who watched it were enchanted that a person, such as the heroine, could be so completely transformed. The way God transforms us, making us fit to be united with him through love, is far more radical and fascinating than the professor's making over this girl to such an extent that he fell in love with her.

What God loves in us, he has put there. Part of our joy in his love is participation in the process by which he changes us to the extent that he can unite himself to us in love. Those who are most conscious of his work of changing them, who humbly recognize that there was not much in them for God to start with, are the ideal subjects for this divine alchemy. We see it again and again, in St. Margaret Mary, St. Benedict Joseph Labre, St. Therese. Going further back, we see it in our Lady herself, whom he prepared by her immaculate conception to be the mother of his Son. In this process we are not passive as statues under the hand of the sculptor. We cooperate freely, and this cooperation is a source of joy.

Our joy in the love of God is increased by a consciousness of the personal element in this love. We make a mistake if we look on our love of God as a theological abstraction. While it is true that we must avoid vapid sentimentality and false emotionalism in connection with our love of the Almighty, he invites us to an intimate union of mind and heart that is astounding. When Christ appeared as a youth to St. Teresa of Avila, and identified himself as *Jesus of Teresa* after she had replied to his question as to her identity that she was *Teresa of Jesus,* he showed that he does not disdain receiving us on the most personal and familiar terms. It is to be observed that Teresa of the towering intellect and supernaturally transpierced heart never allowed this relationship to degenerate into anything unworthy of the divinity. She always referred to our Lord as *His Divine Majesty.*

We are liable to think of this willingness of God's to receive our personal love as something that came in with the New Testament. There is no doubt about the impetus that was given to a deeply personal relationship between God and man by God's becoming man. In the Incarnation, he assumed a human heart, and he himself, through his revelations to St. Margaret Mary, has offered this heart as a symbol of the warmth of his love.

Although the closeness of God has been felt more since his coming into the world as one of us, we cannot fail to be struck by the expressions of God's love for man in the Old Testament. So great was his loving care of the Hebrews that Moses said that he "guarded them as if they had been the apple of his eye" (Deut. 32:10). And Isaias has the Lord saying: "You shall be carried at the breasts and upon the knees . . . ; as one whom the mother caresseth, so will I comfort you" (66:13, CV).

In one breath, David sang of God's splendor and power, and his care for even his inanimate creation: "Does he not know the number of the stars, and call each by its name? How great a Lord is ours, how magnificent his strength, how inscrutable his wisdom. . . . Strike up, then, in thanksgiving to the Lord, with the harp's music praise our God." (Ps. 146:4-7) We moderns picture the billions upon billions of stars in the seemingly limitless universe, and God's interest in each of these stars. Then we think of his loving interest in the apparently tiny creature, for whom the stars and the universe were made, the hairs of whose head are numbered.

If any lingering doubt enters our minds that God wants us to have a joy in loving him that is akin to the joy of human love, the doubt should be eliminated by his having inspired the beloved in the Song of Songs to say of her lover: "The voice I love! See where he comes, how he speeds over the mountains, how he spurns the hills! Gazelle nor fawn was ever so fleet of foot as my heart's love. And now he is standing on the other side of this very wall; now he is looking in through each window in turn, peering through every chink. I can hear my true love calling to me: Rise up, rise up quickly, dear heart. . . ." (2:8-10) Since God has invited this sort of intimate love, we have no reason to deprive ourselves of the joy of it. The joy of heaven will be a result of our union with the God whom we are even commanded to love in this life. There is no reason why there should not be intimations of that eternal joy in our love of him now.

4. *The Joy of Repentance*

Since we wayfaring mortals are all sinners, there are few things more reassuring than God's eagerness to pardon our lapses. No more joyful note is struck in the whole of the Gospels than that which the Son of God sounds when he speaks of the return of the wandering sinner to his Father's house.

Christ tells of the shepherd who loses one of a hundred sheep, and after a search finds it. "And when he does find it, he sets it on his shoulders, rejoicing, and so goes home, and calls his friends and neighbors together; Rejoice with me, he says to them, I have found my sheep that was lost" (Lk. 15:5-6). He even speaks of the rejoicing that goes on in heaven, where we would suppose that fullness of joy would leave no room for further exultation: "So it is, I tell you, in heaven; there will be more rejoicing over one sinner who repents, than over ninety-nine souls that are justified, and have no need for repentance" (Lk. 15:7).

Our Lord uses another illustration to drive home his point, that of the woman who loses, and later finds, one of her ten silver pieces: "If some woman has ten silver pieces by her, and has lost one of them, does she not light a lamp, and sweep the house, and search carefully until she finds it? And when she does find it, she calls her friends and neighbors together; Rejoice with me, she says, I have found the silver piece which I lost. So it is, I tell you, with the angels of God; there is joy among them over one sinner that repents." (Lk. 15:8-10)

The parables of the rejoicing over the recovered sheep and silver piece lead up to that of the prodigal son, which cannot be surpassed for deep and climactic joy. Our Lord says that the younger of two sons asked his father for the share of the estate that would normally go to him at his father's death. Evidently, he told of his plans to establish a business in a distant country, and the father was persuaded by his arguments. Having received the money, he went into that country, wasting what he had received in riotous living. When it was all spent, a famine came upon the place, and he was reduced to feeding swine, not even being allowed to eat the husks that he threw to them. Then he thought of the servants in his father's house, and decided to go back and ask his father to take him in as one of them.

Nothing would have been more natural than for such a father to say, "So you have come back? Come into the house. I forgive you." But this father is representing God receiving back the repentant sinner. Our Lord describes him as recognizing his son in the distance. He does not wait for the son to approach. He rushes up, embraces and kisses him, and hardly allowing him to blurt out his little prepared speech about not being worthy to be called a son, he turns to the servants and gives a series of orders: "Bring out the best robe, and clothe him in it; put a ring on his hand, and shoes on his feet. Then bring out the calf that has been fattened, and kill it; let us eat, and make merry; for my son here was dead, and has come to life again, was lost, and is found." (Lk. 15:22-24)

Christ was only making clear that the reception given the prodigal son is that which awaits the greatest sinner in the world, if he wants to revive his hope and return to the house of his Father. One of the most striking aspects of this parable is that the joy which is emphasized is not that of the repentant son, but of the father who has witnessed his return. This is of great encouragement to the sinner who wonders what kind of a reception he will receive if he decides to return to the sacraments. One who has sinned greatly might think that a priest would be annoyed by having to hear the confession of a person who has been away from the Church for a long time. He should realize that for the average priest there are few joys as great as being the instrument of reconciling another human being with God.

Our joy in receiving God's pardon is increased by the completeness of his forgiveness. How complete that forgiveness is can be seen, not only in the parables recalled in this chapter, but in the many examples of our Lord's forgiveness recorded in the Gospels. His forgiveness of Mary Magdalen, for instance, was so absolute that she is pictured in the Gospels as the first person to whom Christ appeared after the resurrection. We find here no condescension toward the reformed sinner. There is no indication whatsoever that this woman had once been estranged from God. His attitude of forgiving and forgetting, the totality of his pardon, are indicated by the warmth reflected in his one word of greeting when he appeared to her outside the tomb: "Mary."

The other instances of his forgiveness convey a similar joy to us after two thousand years. We picture the woman who had been taken in adultery leaping to her feet when her accusers had left and Christ had pardoned her, her heart pounding with relief and joy. We sense the joy of the woman of Samaria as she puts down her water pot at the well where she has been talking with our Lord, and hurries back to the village to announce breathlessly that she has been talking with the Messias. It is clear that the basis of her joy is the conviction that, since he is the Messias, he can forgive her the transgressions of which he had reminded her in their conversation.

Part of the Church's joy in her saints comes from the fact that not a few of the towering men and women that she has given the world would not be saints at all had not God been ready to forgive their falls. We have only to think of such fallen and restored giants as St. Peter, St. Paul and St. Augustine to see how true this is.

Sometimes those who least need forgiveness have the best understanding of God's readiness to pardon offenses. St. Therese, although a model of sinlessness, could place herself in the position of one guilty of great sin, and realize the joy with which she would be welcomed back. "I am sure," she writes, "that even if I had every imaginable crime on my conscience, I would lose none of my confidence but would cast myself, heartbroken with sorrow, into the arms of my Savior. I recall his love for the prodigal son, I have heard his words to Mary Magdalen, to the woman taken in adultery and the woman of Samaria."

At a time when the fear of nuclear war is so widespread, one naturally thinks of the joy that would come to the world through universal repentance and pardon. The tragic story of war and threats of war which makes the front page of the daily paper so joyless would be reversed if mankind were to return to God. That God is eager to forgive in a universal context is evident from many parts of Scripture.

God offered a reprieve to Sodom in the intriguing conversation that he held with Abraham. The latter asked whether God would spare the city from the destruction with which he had threatened it if fifty innocent men could be found in it. God replied that he would spare it for that many. Abraham, evidently sensing that fifty could not be found, brought the number down to forty-five, then to forty, and after that, to thirty, to twenty, and finally to ten. "I will spare it from destruction to save ten," God assured the patriarch. God does not change. He wants to spare mankind from further chastisement, and will do so if even a relatively small number of godly people can be found. (Gen. 18:23-33)

The joy that would have been Sodom's if it had repented was actually experienced by Nineve, which Scripture calls "a great city indeed." The Ninevites accepted the warning which the prophet Jonas gave them in God's name that the city would be overthrown in forty days. "With that," says the Prophecy of Jonas, "the Ninevites showed faith in God, rich and poor alike, proclaiming a fast and putting on sackcloth; nay, the king of Nineve himself, when word of it reached him, came down from his throne, cast his robe aside, put on sackcloth, and sat down humbly in the dust.

. . . Thus, when God saw them amending their lives in good earnest, he spared them, in his mercy, their threatened punishment." (Jon. 3:2-10)

In our own day, our Lady of Fatima gave the world a message of hope. The joy of being forgiven has been offered just as surely to humanity in this century as it was to Sodom and Nineve. So far, the joy has been forfeited, because mankind has chosen to imitate Sodom rather than Nineve. Great would be the joy on earth and in heaven if the human race were to reach out for the forgiveness constantly held out to it by the God of mercy.

One of the things that rob true servants of God of joy is concern about their small lapses. They wonder whether their failure to overcome even in small things indicates that they are attached to small sins, and, therefore, lack repentance for them. It goes without saying that we are expected to strive to eliminate deliberate venial sins, since these constitute a form of law-breaking. They are violations of God's law, even though minor violations. But we are not to allow small falls to discourage us. The fact that they continue does not indicate that we are not sorry for them.

It is possible that God allows us to fall into minor sins in order to help us grow in the all-important virtue of humility. With charming candor, St. Therese says of such defects: "If only I am humble, if only I am insignificant, I may, without offending God, commit little follies from now until the day of my death. Think of small children. They are for ever breaking and tearing things and tumbling over things; yet, all the time, they love their parents very much and are very much loved by them."

That the joy of repentance for small lapses need not be diminished by their recurrence is indicated in another captivating avowal of this extraordinary saint: "I am much happier on account of my weakness than if, borne up by grace, I had been a model of patience."

All of us, whether we have had great falls or a series of minor falls, can rejoice in the encouraging words that Isaias addresses to all stumbling pilgrims on the road to eternity: "A message from the high God, the great God, whose habitation is eternity, whose name is hallowed! He, dwelling in that high and holy place, dwells also among chastened and humbled souls, bidding the humble spirit, the chastened soul, rise and live! I will not be always claiming my due, I will not cherish my anger eternally; what soul but takes its origin from me? Am I not the maker of all that breathes? Greedy wrong-doer that defies me I must needs smite down; hide my face from him in anger, let him follow the path his own erring will has chosen. Now to pity his plight, now to bring him remedy! Home-coming at last, consolation for him at last, for him and all that bemoan him! The harvest of men's thanks, it is I that bring it to the birth. Peace, the Lord says, peace to those who are far away, and to those who are near at hand. I have brought him remedy." (Is. 57:15-19)

5. *The Joy of Christ in Us*

The beautiful prayer which the Church has the priest offer when he blends the wine and water in the chalice during Mass expresses the main reason for our joy in this world:

O God, who in a marvelous manner didst create and ennoble human nature, and still more wonderfully hast renewed it; grant that, by the mystical union of this water and wine, we may be made partakers of his divinity who vouchsafed to become partaker of our humanity, Jesus Christ, thy Son, our Lord. St. Paul exulted that he had been given "this privilege, of making known to the Gentiles the unfathomable riches of Christ" (Eph. 3:8). It was this sharing in the Godhead, through Christ, that he chiefly had in mind when he referred to the unfathomable riches of the Savior.

Knowing Christ through the Gospels is a source of joy. Hearing and understanding his word also are wellsprings of gladness. But it is doubtful whether we would have been content with just knowing him and his truth. We would have been ready to settle for nothing less than a participation in his very life.

The thrilling fact is that participation in his life means participation in his divinity. Before this truth is considered, it will be helpful to recall how completely we are one with him. Nothing could be closer than the vine and its branches. And he says: "I am the vine, you are its branches" (Jn. 15:6). St. Paul illustrates this oneness between Christ and us by comparing it with the union that exists between head and members in our physical bodies. "Each of us," he says, "has one body, with many different parts . . . ; just so we, though many in number, form one body in Christ" (Rom. 12:4-5). And in another place, he says: "He has put everything under his dominion, and made him the head to which the whole Church is joined, so that the Church is his body, the completion of him who everywhere and in all things is complete" (Eph. 1:22-23). Just as the life that is in the head and members of our natural bodies is one and the same life, so with the life that is in Christ and in us.

As fishes live in the sea, as birds live in the air, we live in Christ. Paraphrasing the words of Scripture, we may say that in him we live, and move, and have our spiritual being. St. Paul says: "Christ Jesus is alive in you" (II Cor. 13:5). At another time, he writes: "For me, life means Christ" (Phil. 1:21). And writing about the way in which he has died to the things of this world, he says: "with Christ I hang upon the cross, and yet I am alive; or rather, not I; it is Christ that lives in me" (Gal. 2:19-20).

So intimate is the union between Christ and us that any spiritual growth can only come through, in, and by him. St. Paul says that we have to "grow up, in everything, into a due proportion with Christ, who is our head. On him all the body depends; it is organized and unified by each contact with the source which supplies it. . . ." (Eph. 4:15-16)

Catholicism is a religion of joy, and the reason is that the life which we have together with Christ is nothing else than the life of the Triune God. Holy Scripture states this without qualification: "you are to share the divine nature" (II Pet. 1:4). And St. Paul talks about the fulfillment of our divine destiny as depending on our Lord's communication of his divine life to us: "In Christ the whole plenitude of Deity is embodied, and dwells in him, and it is in him that you find your completion" (Col. 2:9-10).

The Colossians were warned by St. Paul not to allow anybody to cheat them "by insisting on a false humility which addresses its worship to angels" (Col. 2:18). What he evidently meant was that the idea which we have been developing, that we are partakers of the nature and life of God, might be regarded by those who based their deductions on human logic as being too sublime a destiny for poor fallen human nature. He goes on to say, "Such a man takes his stand upon false visions; his is the ill-founded confidence that comes of human speculation. He is not united to that head of ours, on whom all the body depends, supplied and unified by joint and ligament, and so growing up with a growth which is divine." (2:18-19)

Nothing that we have quoted from Scripture thus far is stronger than the Master's own words in connection with the life that we receive from and through him in the Holy Eucharist: "He who eats my flesh, and drinks my blood, lives continually in me, and I in him. As I live because of the Father, the living Father who has sent me, so he who eats me will live, in his turn, because of me." (Jn. 6:57-58)

Once we have received this divine life through Christ, our souls are transformed. We are not changed in such a way that our identity is affected. It is a change which may be compared with that which takes place in iron when it is made red hot. When heated to this degree, although it preserves its nature as iron, it appears to have taken on the nature of fire. The fire permeates it through and through. A bright luster replaces its dullness, burning heat its coldness, and malleability its natural rigidity. When the life of Christ really takes possession of a soul, it permeates it, makes it aflame with divine truth and goodness, gives it a brightness, which in the case of the saints sometimes shone in their faces, and prepares it to be molded by the divine artisan.

A natural question that arises is why there is not more evidence of this divine life in the members of the Church. The answer is that growth in this life, which is received in baptism and nurtured by the other sacraments and by the practice of virtue, is not automatic. Many in the Church just about keep the flame of this life alive under the ashes of venial sin.

The fact is that Christ and his life can constantly be coming into our lives. Our Lord said that a woman who has given birth forgets all her previous pain for joy that a a man is born into the world. Our joy fundamentally is not only that a Man-God has been born into the world but that he continues to communicate his life to us two thousand years after his coming. He is willing to come in greater degree year after year, month after month, week after week, day after day, but we block his coming through the wall we construct of our venial sins. Our deliberate venial sins are like so many small stones in the wall that keeps Christ out of our lives. Taken separately, they appear somewhat inconsequential. Then, one day, we look up, and we see this wall standing between Christ and us.

Perhaps a good illustration of our general attitude toward Christ is the way in which Christians frequently celebrate Christmas. Their joy reaches a peak once a year on the birthday of Christ. All the lovely Christmas carols are brought out and sung. The world echoes the exultant strain of *Joy to the world—the Lord has come!* Sadly, when the carols are put away, the joy of his coming seems to be put away with them. The joy of his coming is turned on, almost like the lights in our windows and around our doors with which we herald the festive season. As these lights go out during Christmas week, so the light and life of him whose birth they are meant to celebrate are, as it were, turned off.

What Pope Paul said concerning Christ at the reconvening of the Second Vatican Council applies not only to such an historic gathering of Christ's shepherds, but to the daily life of every last member of his sheepfold. Pope Paul said that the Council had to answer three questions: from what point the Bishops were to set out; what road they intended to travel; and what was the goal they proposed to themselves. Magnificently answering these questions, he thus spoke of Christ, our Lord: "These three . . . questions have only one answer, namely, that here and at this very hour we should proclaim Christ to ourselves and to the world around us; Christ our beginning, Christ our life and our guide, Christ our hope and our end."

Particularly significant was his stating that the bishops had to proclaim Christ to themselves. Actually, the Pope included himself by saying, "We should proclaim Christ to *ourselves.*" If he thus expressed the need he felt to remind himself of the centrality of Christ, we lesser members of Christ's Mystical Body do not have to feel embarrassed that we do not recall in every wakeful moment that Christ is, as Pope Paul reminded the Council Fathers, "the Incarnate Word, the Son of God and the Son of Man, the Redeemer of the world, the Hope of humanity and its supreme Master, the Good Shepherd, the Bread of Life, the High Priest and our Victim, the sole Mediator between God and men, the Savior of the world, the eternal King of Ages." It is enough that we have a great desire to keep all these truths concerning Christ in mind, and that we continue to strive that they will be woven into the fabric of our daily lives. We can at least want very deeply to be able one day to say: "There is nothing but Christ in any of us" (Col. 3:11). And we can pray that this desire will indeed be fulfilled before we leave this world, and look up into the countenance of Christ, the eternal Judge. By then, our relationship to him will have been forever determined. All the while before that eventuality, we are to act on the words first addressed to the Colossians: "You are to be rooted in him, built up on him . . ." (2:7).

The life that we have by Christ, with Christ, and in Christ, is called sanctifying grace. If we understood what it means to grow in life in Christ, the only thing that would concern us would be to gain an increase of sanctifying grace every day of our lives. The only thing we would fear would be losing even a small degree of this grace.

If there is mediocrity in our lives, it is because the joy of growing in Christ's life is not understood. When it is understood, growth in it is all that matters. For one who has this understanding, any activity that does not contribute to growth in Christ is fundamentally shallow and futile. We should try to reach the stage where there is only boredom when Christ is left out.

Christ is left out of our actions whenever they are in contradiction to his teaching. He is hardly to be found in the irreverent use of his name, in the sharp or angry word, or in detracting or lying speech. We cannot be surprised that Christ stays out of the heart that gives lodging to proud or lustful thoughts.

In explaining the practical aspects of life in Christ to the Colossians, St. Paul said: "But now he [God] has used Christ's natural body to win you back through his death, and so bring you into his presence, holy, spotless, and unreproved. But that means that you must be true to your faith, grounded in it, firmly established in it." (Col. 1:22-23)

It is Christ and the life that he communicates to us which explains why the Catholic who gives himself totally to the practice of his faith possesses within himself a wellspring of joy. This is what makes him glad to the point of exultation. This is what makes the convert to the Church act as one who has found a great treasure, which indeed he has.

This life of Christ which we have in time is only the beginning. The strong, rich life of our divine Savior, the life of the Triune God, is pulsating through our souls, preparing us for the glorious consummation of his Kingdom in the world to come.

Christ is not only the arch that spans the abyss between God and man, he is not only the Way, the Truth, the Life and the Resurrection; he is also the splendor of the Kingdom which will begin when this world is swallowed up in eternity. Christ is not only the beginning of our Christian life but also its end. He is Omega as well as Alpha.

When we realize the joy that flows from life in Christ, we find a special savor in the words with which the Church closes so many of her official prayers: *through Jesus Christ, thy Son, our Lord.* For one who possesses Christ, and is possessed by him, these words are honey to his mouth, music to his ears, joy to his heart.

It was the thought of this great mystery that prompted St. Paul's eloquent words to the Colossians: "May all the wealth of Christ's inspiration have its shrine among you; now you will have instruction and advice for one another, full of wisdom, now there will be psalms, and hymns, and spiritual music, as you sing with gratitude in your hearts to God. Whatever you are about, in word and action alike, invoke always the name of the Lord Jesus Christ, offering your thanks to God the Father through him." (3:16-17) "Christ is your life," he writes, "and when he is made manifest, you too will be made manifest in glory with him" (3:4).

6. *The Joy of Sons*

Christ took upon himself our human nature in order to become our elder Brother. Because he is our Brother, we are the sons of God. In writing of our adoption by God as his sons, St. Augustine quoted a pagan philosopher who said that it would be a great boon to a nation if its citizens were convinced that they were the descendants of gods. The philosopher had in mind the extraordinary efforts that such citizens would be willing to make to be worthy of such exalted origin. It is evident also that such an illusion, if accepted wholeheartedly, would be the source of great, if deceptive, satisfaction and joy.

Our joy as sons and daughters of God is based on no fable or illusion. We have the word of God himself that he has adopted us. St. Paul explains this divine adoption to the Galatians: "Then God sent out his Son on a mission to us. He took birth from a woman, took birth as a subject of the law, so as to ransom those who were subject to the law, and make us sons by adoption. To prove that you are sons, God has sent out the Spirit of his Son into your hearts, crying out in us, Abba, Father. No longer, then, art thou a slave, thou art a son." (4:4-7)

To adopt a child means to introduce, of one's own free will, a stranger into one's family, and to confer on him the title of son, with all the advantages connected therewith, especially the right of inheritance. This right of the sons of God is stressed by St. Paul when he says: "and because thou art a son, thou hast, by divine appointment, the son's right of inheritance" (Gal. 4:7).

The important effects that may follow adoption in earthly life are illustrated in the life of the Roman Emperor Trajan. He had been a mere soldier of fortune, a stranger bearing no relationship to the family of the Caesars. He owed his high station solely to his adoption by the Emperor Nerva. The gift of adoption would have been all the greater in the case of Trajan, if he had been a slave before his adoption. This is the position we were in when adopted by God.

In considering our adoption by God, it should be emphasized that only the Eternal Word is the Son of God by nature. Before our adoption, our relationship to God was that of creature to Creator. Creatures by nature, we became strangers to him by sin. Sanctifying grace raised us from the position of creatures and strangers to that of sons. Through grace, we have become sharers in the glory and privileges of the only-begotten Son.

We are now free to address the sovereign Lord of heaven and earth with the endearing title, Father. Although our Lord commanded us to address God in this way when he taught us the *Our Father,* the Church reminds us what an august privilege this is by the words with which she prefaces the offering of this perfect prayer in the Mass: *Taught by thy saving precepts, and following the divine command, we make bold to say: Our Father. . . .*

As though to leave no doubt in our minds that we are in reality the sons of God, Christ, after his resurrection, told Mary Magdalen to give his disciples this message: "I am going up to him who is my Father and your Father

. . ." (Jn. 20:17). He says "my Father and your Father" because there is a difference between the way in which he is Son by nature and we are sons by adoption. But the intimate manner in which he links the two terms shows that we are indeed the sons of God.

That the joy of this marvelous truth remained fresh for the Apostles is revealed in the brisk way in which St. John, for instance, writes in one of his epistles: "See how the Father has shown his love towards us; that we should be counted as God's sons, should be his sons" (I Jn. 3:1). He says that we are not just counted as God's sons, but are really such, to make clear that, unlike earthly adoption, our adoption by God actually constitutes us sons. Legal adoption confers only exterior advantages. It is powerless to transmit to the adopted child anything of the nature or life of the one adopting. A man could not give a child whom he adopts a participation in his nature, regardless of how greatly he might desire to do so.

What is impossible to man is possible to God. In adopting man, God gives him a share in his very nature and life. "You are to share the divine nature," says St. Peter (II Pet. 1:4). Through sanctifying grace, there is in us a real regeneration, a sharing in the life of the Godhead. Having been born in the natural order of the flesh of our parents, we are born in the supernatural order through grace. It is to this second birth that St. Peter is referring when he says: ". . . you have all been born anew with an immortal, imperishable birth" (I Pet. 1:23). St. John links this birth with belief in Christ: "But all those who did welcome him, he empowered to become the children of God, all those who believe in his name; their birth came, not from human stock, not from nature's will or man's, but from God" (1:12-13).

There is always something pathetic in a joy which is based on illusion. The reason is that when the illusion is shattered, the joy will also be. There is a great deal of this kind of joy in the world, and many of those who indulge in it would resent any attempt to destroy their illusions. One of the obligations of those who possess the truth is to attempt to show that joy in the divine adoption rests on the established truth that the Eternal Father, who communicates his nature to his Son substantially from all eternity, communicates it to us accidentally in time.

St. Paul observes that we who have been baptized in Christ's name "have put on the person of Christ" (Gal. 3:27). When we have put on the person of Christ, the Father extends to us the love which he has for his incarnate Son. It is because his Son is in us that the Father can have for us also a father's love. This is why our elder Brother could pray at the Last Supper: "I have revealed, and will reveal, thy name to them; so that the love thou hast bestowed upon me may dwell in them, and I, too, may dwell in them" (Jn. 17:26).

Our joy is increased by the consciousness that God did not just make us his sons, and then put us completely on our own resources. Every father wants his children to be a credit to him and to themselves. For this reason, he provides them with every available opportunity for development, intellectual, social and spiritual. But the most devoted earthly father's interest in the welfare of his children is naturally only an imitation of our heavenly Father's all-embracing interest in everything that concerns us.

In his indescribable love for us, God bestows on us every grace and gift that will help us to be worthy sons and a credit to the greatest of fathers. He begins by giving us faith, that we may believe everything that our Father has said. He adds hope, that we may have unwavering trust in his constant support and unfailing reward. He infuses love into our souls, that we may love our heavenly Father first and above all, and his other children because they are his children.

To this trinity of divine gifts, he joins four others. He bestows justice, that we may give God and all his children their due. He adds prudence, that we may act with the good sense of worthy sons. He gives fortitude, that we may not be weak or cowardly sons, but courageous ones. To these he joins temperance, to help us use our Father's gifts without excess. Rich and loving Father that he is, God adds special gifts, called the gifts of his Spirit: wisdom, understanding, counsel, fortitude, knowledge, piety, and fear of him. All these help us to understand our heavenly Father's purpose, make us more attentive to his voice, more ready to receive his grace, more docile to his divine impulses.

Often in earthly life, a powerful motive for proper living is found in coming from a family that has established a reputation for probity. Those who are of the family of God should only have to say to themselves in time of temptation: *A son of God could not do that!*

It is not, however, merely a question of avoiding what is unbecoming in children of such a Father. A father is certainly not satisfied if his children just stay out of trouble. He wants them to accomplish something of which both he and they can rightly be proud. God is surely not less demanding than an earthly father in regard to his children measuring up to the high standards that he has set for them.

We forfeit the joy of sons if we fail to qualify as worthy

sons. Not only do we deprive ourselves of joy through such failure, but we deprive our Father of the glory that is given him when his sons live righteously. Furthermore, we fail to show our unbelieving fellowman the joy that could be his by becoming a son of God.

If the president of a corporation had his sons elected to the board of directors, naturally those acquainted with the family would watch to see whether the sons would justify their father's trust. The world watches Catholics in a similar way. Although it knows little, or nothing, about our claim to be sons of God and brothers of Christ, it is vaguely conscious of our conviction that we bear a special relationship to God. It expects this relationship to show itself in a better than average practice of justice, prudence, fortitude, and temperance. Just as good-willed relatives and friends of the father who brought his sons into his company would feel disappointed if the sons betrayed their father's trust, non-Catholics of good will must experience a similar feeling when Catholics fail to justify the special position to which they claim to have been raised.

Many outside the Church are sincerely searching for the truth, often watching us out of the corner of their eyes, perhaps hoping that we will prove, by our conduct, that there is something to our exalted claims. When they are confronted with someone who has really proven himself to be a son of God, they make no effort to conceal their satisfaction and joy. This explains the unique impact of Pope John XXIII. No person of our time has brought more joy to the world than this worthy son of our heavenly Father.

The eternal joy and glory which our Father has destined for us will be ours if we heed the counsel of St. Paul: "As God's favored children, you must be like him"

(Eph. 5:1). The Apostle was paraphrasing the injunction already given by our elder Brother: "But you are to be perfect, as your heavenly Father is perfect" (Matt. 5:48).

The rounding out of our destiny as sons is beautifully developed by St. Paul in his Epistle to the Romans: "If creation is full of expectancy, that is because it is waiting for the sons of God to be made known . . . nature in its turn will be set free from the tyranny of corruption, to share in the glorious freedom of God's sons" (8:19, 21).

7. The Joy of Brothers

When Christ became our elder Brother by assuming our human nature, he made us sons of God, and brothers, one of another. In writing about our joy in the Church, we quoted St. Paul's development of the truth of our oneness in the Mystical Body of Christ. "A man's body is all one," he says, "though it has a number of different organs; and all this multitude of organs goes to make up one body; so is it with Christ. We too, all of us, have been baptized into a single body. . . ." (I Cor. 12:12, 13) Just as it is a joy to contemplate the marvelous harmony and cooperation that exist among our physical members, there is joy at the sight of unity and mutual assistance among the members that Christ has joined to himself and to one another.

The members of our bodies are always working for each other's benefit. If the hand could think and feel, we can imagine the satisfaction it would experience in lifting food to the mouth, and thus nourishing the entire body. In a similar way, any member of Christ's body who has his spirit of love experiences a deep joy in serving the other members of his body. So great was St. Paul's joy in serving his brethren that he wrote in one of his epistles: "What thanks can we return to God for you, to express all the joy we feel in rejoicing over you in the presence of our God, as we pray more than ever, night and day, for the opportunity of seeing you face to face, and making good whatever your faith still lacks?" (I Thess. 3:9, 10).

Our bodily members seem almost to feel satisfaction in coming to the aid of an injured member. If the foot should be bruised or wounded, the hands lift the hurt member, the head is lowered that the eyes may examine the injury, and the fingers apply a healing and antiseptic remedy. A similar phenomenon is often observed in Christ's body, the Church. A good illustration is the joy with which a truly dedicated member of the Church will work day and night to bring healing to the physically or spiritually sick.

The marvelous reflexes that exist among the members for the defense of the body are also a joy to see. If a blow is aimed at the face, all the members try to ward it off. The hands are raised to shield the face, the feet draw the body back to a safe distance from the assailant. It is also a source of joy when the members of the Church come to the assistance of any member that is threatened, whether the threat be in the physical or the spiritual order.

The cooperation among our physical members is instinctive. The love that Christ expects among his members can only exist if they make a conscious effort to remember that they are all indeed one with him and with each other. So real is this unity that our Lord tells us that when we appear before him for our final accounting, he will judge as having been done for or to him whatever we have done for or to one another.

Those who have lived by this truth have always brought great joy to their fellowmen. We have only to think of a man like St. Francis to see how true this is. Seven hundred years after his death, St. Francis is still exercising a joyous influence on mankind. The primary reason is that he had a love for others that was as closely patterned on that of Christ as any love has ever been.

The saints were all noted for their wholehearted love of others. St. Benedict wrote in his Rule: "Let every stranger be received as if he were Christ himself, for it is Christ who will one day say to us: 'I was a stranger and you took me in.' " St. Teresa of Avila addressed to priests a plea for this love which every member of the Church might take as addressed to himself: "Christ has no body now on earth but yours, no hands but yours; yours are the eyes through which Christ's compassion is to look out on the world; yours are the feet with which he is to go about doing good, and yours are the hands with which he is to bless us now."

Ours is the joy of having Christ's love for men pass through us to them. We are the channels of his love. It is our high privilege to manifest it to all with whom we live or associate. It is also our grave responsibility to make certain that the love which we give to others is really his love, that it bears the authentic qualities of the love that he showed others during his earthly life.

We will not bring his love to our fellowman unless he sees in it the warm personal interest which our Lord showed, for instance, by calling those with whom he spoke by name. He said to Zacchaeus, the chief publican of Jericho who had climbed a sycamore tree to catch sight of him: "Zacchaeus, make haste and come down; I am to lodge today at thy house" (Lk. 19:5). When Mary Magdalen was asked by the risen Christ why she was weeping, and for whom she was searching in the garden of the sepulchre, and she thought it must be the gardener speaking to her, he revealed his identity with the one word: "Mary" (Jn. 20:15).

To Thomas, who had been absent when he first appeared to the Apostles after the resurrection, and believed only when he saw him on his second appearance, our Lord said: "Thou hast learned to believe, Thomas, because thou hast seen me" (Jn. 20:29). Before giving Peter his commission as Prince of the Apostles, Jesus said to him: "Simon Peter, Simon, son of John, dost thou care for me more than these others?" (Jn. 21:15) Or he would address those with whom he did not have this close personal relationship with the title of *son,* or *daughter.*

Another characteristic of his love that his members have to cultivate, if they are to convey the joy of it, is its prompt generosity. A leper has only to say: "If it be thy will, thou hast power to make me clean." Jesus reaches out his hand, touches him, and says: "It is my will; be thou made clean." (Mk. 1:40-41) Seeing the faith of those who had stripped the tiles from the roof to let down a man afflicted with palsy, he says: "Rise up, take thy bed with thee, and walk" (Mk. 2:9).

A centurion tells Christ that he feels unworthy to receive him under his roof, and that our Lord can cure his valued servant by a word of command, and the centurion returns home to find his servant cured. A blind man sitting by the roadside, and hearing the multitude accompanying Jesus passing by, has but to cry out: "Jesus, Son of David, have pity on me," and our Lord gives him back his sight (Lk. 18:38).

If any member of Christ's body is going to restore the joy of his love to a fallen brother, our Lord wants him to do it without any air of condescension. Otherwise, he will not really be manifesting the love of Christ, who ate with publicans and sinners. There was no condescension when he allowed the sinful Magdalen to wash his feet. There was no trace of it in the conversation he held with the woman at the well in Samaria, a woman who had had five husbands. As the woman came up to draw water, he said: "Give me some to drink." This amazed her, even though she did not know she was speaking with the Messias. She was surprised that he would speak to her, because the Jews despised the Samaritans. Puzzled by his lack of racial prejudice, she asked: "How is it that thou, who art a Jew, dost ask me, a Samaritan, to give thee drink?" (Jn. 4:9) Further conversation with him pretty well convinced her that she was talking with the Christ. We catch the joy of her excitement as she puts down her water-pot and rushes into the city to spread the good news.

The joy that is felt by those who are animated by Christ's spirit of mercy and pity is apparent in the vibrant words of St. Bernadine: "If God should call me to account in judgment for being too severe and inflexible, I should have nothing to answer for myself in defense; but if he should accuse me of being too clement and merciful, I should find an excuse instantly: for I could reply that I had learned mercy from him who had also exceeded measure in showing pity."

Only in eternity will we know the joy that has come to humanity through the practice of what we call the Golden Rule, so bright a guide is it for the bestowal of Christ's love on our fellowman. "Do to other men," he says, "all that you would have them do to you" (Matt. 7:12). We know, he is telling us, what brings us joy from others: generosity, considerateness, thoughtfulness, courtesy, patience, cheerfulness, sympathy. He is showing us further that if we find gladness in a manifestation of these qualities in those who are fellow-pilgrims on the road to heaven, they find gladness in discovering them in us.

An anonymous writer has expressed beautifully the effects that would follow a universal application of the law of love in the Church: "How glorious the vineyard of the Lord would be, how great its appeal, how irresistible its attraction, if all the branches bore this noble fruit of the Spirit."

Christ found a pretext for speaking to the woman at the well in Samaria. He asked her to give him some of the water that she was drawing, in order that he might give her the living water of his grace. How often we do the opposite, looking for pretexts to avoid offering our spiritual brothers and sisters a word of greeting, or of counsel, or of sympathy, or of encouragement. We are surrounded by people who have as great a spiritual thirst as the woman of Samaria, and we fail too frequently to give the water which Christ has given us. We hoard the living water which he wants us to dispense, thus depriving ourselves of the joy of giving, and our fellowman of the joy of receiving.

Perhaps the most striking phenomenon of our times has been the breaking down of the barriers that have separated Catholics and Protestants for more than four centuries. The reciprocal expression of esteem and affection between those who had almost appeared to be enemies has been staggering. The joy that has followed such a relaxation of tensions has swept over mankind like a refreshing wave.

The most remarkable aspect of this situation is that the love and joy that have been manifested were released by the quiet action of one man who reached the conclusion that since we are brothers, we should act as brothers. Pope John XXIII brought more joy to humanity than any man within living memory because he brought more love. He could walk into a room and say with complete naturalness to a group of Jewish brethren who had come to pay their respects: "I am Joseph, your brother." Here was a typical demonstration of love by this extraordinary man, one calculated to bring joy not only to those who were present during the audience, but to all who heard of it. We are reminded of the joy that overflowed from the reunion of the biblical Joseph with his brethren: "And now the news was in everybody's mouth, and all Pharao's court heard that Joseph's brethren were there. Pharao rejoiced heartily over it, and all his courtiers with him." (Gen. 45:16)

A description written by Monsignor Gay years ago of *the face of love* finds a startling fulfillment in Pope John XXIII: "Its brow is serene, its look ingenuous, calm, benevolent, sweet, compassionate, full of attraction; its lips parted, ready to smile, its ear easily inclined; its voice sympathetic; it exhales simplicity and peace like sweet perfume; itself at ease, it makes others so." There is nothing which draws people to God more than to see the light of God's love in the faces of those who claim to be his spokesmen. One thinks of the words of Scripture: "I give thanks to God that he is. . . . through us spreading abroad everywhere, like a perfume, the knowledge of himself" (II Cor. 2:14).

It is said of St. Francis de Sales, Bishop of Geneva, that he brought into the Church seventy thousand of his separated brethren. His outstanding characteristic seems to have been amiability. The prayer of the office and Mass of his feast says of him that, like St. Paul, he became all things to all men.

One test of the depth of our love of others is whether we rejoice when they receive blessings that we would welcome for ourselves, when they are able to do things that we would enjoy doing. It is a question of whether we are convinced that no man is an island to himself, that the sorrow of one is the sorrow of all, and that the joy of one is the joy of all.

When we have reached the stage where we get as much joy from sending letters as we do from receiving them, we can be convinced that we really believe it is more blessed to give than to receive. When we experience a family joy in blessings that come to members of the family of man who are personally unknown to us, we can feel that we have at least begun to practice the love of others that Christ had in mind when he said: "This is my commandment, that you should love one another, as I have loved you" (Jn. 15:12).

8. The Joy of the Holy Spirit

The preface of the Mass is the hymn of praise and thanksgiving which immediately precedes the most sacred part of the holy Sacrifice. The preface varies according to the season, or the feast, which the Church is commemorating. No preface, not even that of Christmas, strikes a more joyous note than that of the Holy Spirit. This is the preface which is used in the Masses of Pentecost and its octave, as well as in what are called votive Masses of the Holy Spirit.

Because we will now be recalling the reasons we have for exulting in the presence of the Holy Spirit in our souls, and in the Church, we quote here the text of this hymn of joy: *It is truly meet and just, right and availing unto salvation, that we should at all times and in all places give thanks to thee, O holy Lord, Father Almighty, everlasting God: through Christ, our Lord: who going up above all the heavens, and sitting on thy right hand, sent forth the Holy Spirit, as he had promised, on the children of adoption. Wherefore does the whole world rejoice with exceedingly great joy all the earth over; and the hosts above and the angelic powers also join in singing the hymn of thy glory. . . .*

It is no accident that this preface particularly has so joyful a ring. In writing about our joy as sons of God, we quoted St. Paul as saying that we are his sons because he "has sent out the Spirit of his Son into your hearts" (Gal. 4:7). In treating of Christ's life within us, we stressed the Apostle's constant use of such phrases as: "Christ Jesus is alive in you"; "it is Christ that lives in me" (II Cor. 13:5, Gal. 2:20). Now we must consider the truth that Christ is alive in us because his Spirit is in us. While St. Paul says that "your bodies belong to the body of Christ," he also says that "your bodies are the shrines of the Holy Spirit" (I Cor. 6:15, 19). Again he says that "a man cannot belong to Christ unless he has the Spirit of Christ" (Rom.

8:9). Spirit in this last quotation is capitalized because the word refers to the Third Person of the Holy Trinity.

It is because there is a lack of understanding of the place of the Holy Spirit in our lives, and in that of the life of the Church, that we do not have a greater participation in that joy which Holy Scripture declares to be one of the fruits of the Spirit. The simple fact is that everything that is accomplished in us is accomplished by the Holy Spirit. All grace, every virtue, every gift, must be ascribed to the Spirit of God. Christ won all for us. All that we receive, we receive through his merits. And yet, every movement of our souls toward God, beginning with the grace to believe, comes from God's Spirit. St. Paul says that "it is only through the Holy Spirit that anyone can say, Jesus is Lord" (I Cor. 12:3).

The very joy of Christ's coming is based on the action of the Spirit. Long before our Lord's birth, Isaias indicated the part that the Holy Spirit would have in his incarnation. "One shall be born," the prophet declared, "on whom the Spirit of the Lord will rest" (Is. 11:2). It was in saying this that he told his hearers that the expected Messias would possess what we now call the seven gifts of the Holy Spirit.

We find further indication of the action of the Third Person in the Incarnation in the Angel Gabriel's reply to our Lady when the joyful news was announced to her that she was to be the mother of the Savior. She asked how this could be since she had vowed virginity. The angel answered: "the Holy Spirit will come upon thee" (Lk. 1:35).

When our Lord left Galilee to begin his public ministry, that brief three-year period of preaching and manifesting of his divinity which has brought so much joy to humanity during the past two thousand years, on arrival in Judea he immediately went to the Jordan to be baptized by John. St. Matthew says that, as our Lord came out of the water, "He saw the Spirit of God coming down like a dove and resting upon him . . ." (3:16). The Holy Spirit also enters into that mysterious temptation which our Savior willed to submit to after his forty-day fast in the desert. "And now Jesus was led by the Spirit away into the wilderness," says the evangelist, "to be tempted there by the devil" (4:1).

The all-embracing action of the Holy Spirit in the Church was indicated to the Apostles by Christ when he told them of the coming of the Spirit after he had ascended to heaven. There is an atmosphere of joyous expectancy in his references to this advent. He had prepared them remotely for the Holy Spirit's coming when he said to them at the Last Supper: "It will be for him, the truth-giving Spirit, when he comes, to guide you into all truth" (Jn. 16:13). Now, after his resurrection, there is a certain breathlessness in the way he tells them not to leave Jerusalem, "but to wait there for the fulfillment of the Father's promise" (Acts 1:4). He explains that the fulfillment of this promise is "a baptism with the Holy Spirit which you are to receive, not many days from this" (5). When the Apostles, still showing a certain worldly attitude, asked whether he planned to restore Israel's earthly glory, he patiently replied: "Enough for you, that the Holy Spirit will come upon you, and you will receive strength from him" (8).

When the great day of promise arrived, the joy of the Apostles was as close to being ecstatic as any joy in this world could be. Holy Scripture speaks of a sound coming from heaven like that of a strong wind blowing. "Then appeared to them what seemed to be tongues of fire, which parted and came to rest on each of them; and they were all filled with the Holy Spirit . . ." (Acts 2:3-4). It is regrettable that so many in the Church fail to receive from the liturgy the sense of awesome joy which the Church expresses in the celebration of Pentecost. There are only two weeks in the entire year when the Church concentrates her whole liturgical arrangement and spirit on mysteries of the Faith. These are Easter week and Pentecost week. Not only does she forbid the observance of the feast of any saint at those times, but even a commemoration of a saint in the Mass or office. In this way she calls the attention of those of her members who are alert enough to notice, the profound significance of our Lord's resurrection and his sending of the Holy Spirit.

The marvelous effects of the Spirit on our lives are demonstrated in the change which his coming wrought in the Apostles. Easter night the doubting Apostles had locked the doors of the room in which they had assembled "for fear of the Jews" (Jn. 20:19). When they had received the Holy Spirit, less than two months later, they preached with such courage and conviction that three thousand men were converted the day of Pentecost alone. And after they had miraculously cured the man lame from birth at the gate of the temple, and were summoned before the Jewish leaders, their courage amazed their interrogators. Scripture says of these officials that, "seeing the boldness of Peter and John, and discovering that they were simple men, without learning, they were astonished" (Acts 4:13).

We have the joy of knowing that the Holy Spirit is ready and waiting to change us in ways similar to those in which he changed the Apostles. He is still the principle of life for the Mystical Body of Christ, as the soul is the principle of life for the physical body. He is ever eager to pass over the waiting minds and hearts of men, like those warm winds of spring that stir the dormant life of tree, flower and seeded ground.

The Spirit is continually hovering over the Church, ready to descend with those graces and gifts which he alone can bring. He is only waiting for us to say, *Come, Holy Spirit,* to expand our souls with the joy that is an intimation of the joy of eternal life.

The forces set in motion by the Second Vatican Council have been a manifestation of the spiritual forces that the Holy Spirit is constantly prepared to exert in the Church. We members of the Mystical Body of Christ in the mid-twentieth century have had the joy of seeing a new coming of the Spirit of God. We have all been witnesses of another Pentecost, when the Holy Spirit has descended on a multitude of prelates of various races, nations and ages.

An important aspect of the action of the Holy Spirit in the Ecumenical Council is that the holding of it was not automatic. No council had been held in almost a century, and even some of the bishops were not in favor of calling it. Another century could have passed without one. But the man whom the Spirit of God had set over the Church said in his heart, *Come, Holy Spirit.* And the Spirit quietly inspired him to convoke a council.

The Church will never be the same after the Council. Even apart from decrees issued under the authority of the Council Fathers, and the impact of these decrees on the life of the Church, the whole world has witnessed the gathering of two and a half thousand bishops who can trace their office back almost two thousand years to the twelve men chosen by the Son of God to establish his

Church. As a result of the prayer of one man who said, *Come, Holy Spirit,* there has been a world-wide discussion of religious truths and practices unparalleled in human history. A veritable flood of lectures, conversations, articles and books bears out the truth that the Spirit only needs to be invoked to awaken the souls of those who desire to experience his divine action.

Considering the vital spiritual forces unleashed by the Council, we recall the words of Genesis, "over its waters, stirred the breath of God" (1:2). We think also of the words of the Acts of the Apostles, "and they were all filled with the Holy Spirit" (2:4). Because life is a thing of joy, and a surge of life has swept through the Church, there comes to mind also the exultant phrase of the preface of the Holy Spirit, "wherefore does the whole world rejoice, with exceedingly great joy all the earth over."

Nothing could be more important, in considering the action of the Holy Spirit, than that he must act through individual members of the Church, from the pope and the bishops down to the most obscure members of the laity. There is a tendency to think of the Church as a sprawling, bureaucratic organization, rather than as the pulsating organism that it is. The Church is made up of individual souls, who when taken together are the *People of God.* It is of the individual person that Scripture speaks when it says that "a man cannot belong to Christ unless he has the Spirit of Christ" (Rom. 8:9).

Because the Spirit can act only through individual members, it is necessary for each of us to place himself under the influence of the Holy Spirit. Each member of the Mystical Body, whether he be pope, bishop, priest, monk, nun, statesman, scientist, artist, physician, engineer, business man, housewife, or student, has to cry,

Come, Holy Spirit. The Church is holy with the unique holiness of its Head, Christ, but the work of the Mystical Body on earth depends on the zeal of its members. Our contribution to the holiness of the whole Church will depend on the extent to which we allow the Holy Spirit to take over our lives.

Nobody can be a worthy son of the Father, or a recognizable brother of Christ, unless he is guided, strengthened and inspired by him who is the Spirit of the Father and the Son. "Those who follow the leading of God's Spirit are all God's sons," says Holy Scripture (Rom. 8:14).

A great part of the discontent characterizing earthly life comes from a consciousness of life's inequalities. But here is one area where the simplest member of the Church has equal opportunity with the pope. The history of the Church proves that in this question of being influenced in the way of grace and holiness by the Spirit of God the Church is the only truly classless society in the world. Persons who have been obscure—intellectually, economically, socially—have been canonized, and some men who have been raised to the Chair of Peter have been personally unworthy. The fact that they were unworthy did not diminish their juridical authority, but it did diminish the personal inspiration that should have flowed into the Church because of their high office.

During the Ecumenical Council, the bishops discussed the role of the laity in the Church, the function of priests, and even their own powers as the successors of the Apostles. No matter how the functions of the different ranks in the Church are defined, the principal obligation of membership in the Mystical Body of Christ will always be growth in that holiness which is primarily the work of

God's Spirit. If this is lacking, there will be activity without vital action, movement without life.

"Vain is the builder's toil, if the house is not of the Lord's building," says the psalmist; "vainly the guard keeps watch, if the city has not the Lord for its guardian" (Ps. 126:1). Catholic presses may heave, roar and produce; the air waves may be filled with Catholic voices; meetings, conventions and congresses may bear the Catholic name; but if the Spirit of God is not breathing over the waters, all the activity is wasted.

After saying that Christ is the only foundation on which we can build, St. Paul says that "on this foundation different men will build in gold, silver, precious stones, wood, grass, or straw, and each man's workmanship will be plainly seen" (I Cor. 3:12-13). We will build well only if we are guided by the Master Builder, the Holy Spirit, and if he supplies the right materials. Without him, we are left with nothing but the grass and straw of our unaided human efforts. His are the precious materials, wood, priceless stones, silver and gold—the divine graces and gifts which he bestows so lavishly on those who place themselves under his direction.

"Do you not understand that you are God's temple, and that God's Spirit has his dwelling in you?" St. Paul asked the Corinthians (I Cor. 3:16). One of the reasons we do not have more joy in such overwhelming truths of our religion as the indwelling of the Holy Spirit is that we take them for granted. And because we take for granted such a momentous reality as the presence within us of the Spirit of God, we fail to keep "this temple of God which is nothing other than yourselves," cleansed and adorned as becomes such an exalted dwelling (I Cor. 3:17). We are taught by the liturgy, and it is significant that both the secret and postcommunion prayers of the Mass of Pentecost ask that the Spirit purify our hearts. The secret prayer petitions that God "cleanse our hearts by the light of the Holy Spirit," and the postcommunion prayer asks "that the outpouring of the Holy Spirit cleanse our hearts."

The joyous sequence of the Mass of Pentecost calls the Spirit "the soul's delightful guest, the pilgrim's sweet relief." Whether he is to us personally all that this sequence portrays him as being will depend on the extent to which we have acted on the counsel of Holy Scripture: "Let your contentment be in the Holy Spirit; your tongues unloosed in psalms and hymns and spiritual music, as you sing and give praise to the Lord in your hearts" (Eph. 5:18-19).

9. *The Joy of the Church*

The essential reason for our joy in the Church is given by St. Ambrose in one trenchant phrase: "Where the Church is, there is no death, but life eternal." Cardinal Newman, who found the Church after so many years of earnest search, showed that he was transported with joy in discovering her. With an eloquence born of his gladness, he spoke of her thus: "Oh, long sought after, tardily found, desire of the eyes, joy of the heart, the truth after many shadows, the fullness after many foretastes, the home after many storms. . . ."

Christ could have communicated the divine life that he won for mankind directly, but he chose to do so through his Mystical Body. The Church was conceived when he, the Head, was conceived in the womb of Mary. He became Head of the human race through the Incarnation. But the Head is incomplete without the members. This means that, in some mysterious way, the members were united with him when he took flesh of the Virgin Mother. "We are limbs of his body; flesh and bone, we belong to him" (Eph. 5:30).

The Church was born when it sprang from the open side of the Savior on the Cross. It was at that moment that the water and blood flowed to wash and nourish those destined to be members of his Mystical Body. The Church did not appear visibly, however, until the day of Pentecost, when the Holy Spirit opened the floodgates of grace, allowing the torrent of the divine life that Christ had won for us to pour into the souls of men.

St. Paul describes the Church in this way: "A man's body is all one, though it has a number of different organs; and all this multitude of organs goes to make up one body; so it is with Christ. We too, all of us, have been baptized into a single body by the power of a single Spirit." (I Cor. 12:12) A person would have to be extremely dull not to experience a thrill of joy at the sight of Michelangelo's magnificent figure of Adam on the ceiling of the Sistine Chapel. The satisfaction that comes to mind and eye on viewing Adam's perfectly proportioned body seems to be a reflection of the gratification that the great artist put into the countenance of the Almighty as he brings into being this masterpiece of his creation. A comparable feeling of joy is experienced in mind and heart when we contemplate another, and far greater, masterpiece of God's creation, the Mystical Body of Christ, the Church.

Just as the human body is not a haphazard collection of elements, but a marvelous and beautiful arrangement of diverse parts, the Church also is a wonderful and harmonious arrangement of different members.

We take the harmony among the members of our physical bodies for granted. But when we stop to consider this harmony, there is satisfaction in observing the way in which the members of the body perform their separate functions, while working together for the good of the body as a whole. The head thinks for the body, directing the various movements of the members. The eyes are ever on watch, the ears always at their listening posts. The hands supply nourishment to the entire body, the feet carry it wherever the head directs.

There is a deeper joy, because more spiritual, for the Catholic when he considers the way in which Christ, the Head, thinks for his body, the Church. We find joy in the fact that he has given the Church a visible head, who is called his Vicar. He, the supreme Bishop, and the other bishops with him, are the eyes that watch for the Church, the ears that listen for it, the tongue that speaks for it.

The Church rejoices in her prelates because they are the visible representatives of her invisible Head. St. Paul writes of the visible hierarchy in the Church to the Ephesians: "But each of us has received his own special grace, dealt out to him by Christ's gift. . . . Some he has appointed to be apostles, others to be prophets, others to be evangelists, or pastors, or teachers. They are to order the lives of the faithful, minister to their needs, build up the frame of Christ's body, until we all realize our common unity through faith in the Son of God, and fuller knowledge of him." (4:7, 11-13)

The bishops, as successors of the Apostles, participate more intimately in Christ's threefold role as Teacher,

King and Priest. They are united with him in teaching his truth, in ruling his Mystical Body and in sanctifying it.

What it means to the Church to have a supreme shepherd, representing the Divine Shepherd in this world, is illustrated by the wave of joy which sweeps over the Catholic world when the cardinals, gathered in conclave, have elected a new supreme pontiff. All over the earth the members of the Church wait breathlessly for the appearance of the prelate who will go to the balcony of St. Peter's Basilica and proclaim in solemn and joyous tones: *Habemus Papam, We have a Pope!* Anybody who has been in a parish when the bishop of the diocese is expected for the administration of the sacrament of confirmation knows that the air of joyous expectancy is something that would never be found if it were a temporal superior who was awaited.

Further joy is brought to the Church through her world-encircling priesthood. Few rituals are accompanied by a greater air of gladness than the ordination of priests. The spirited way in which Catholics generally greet a priest with the title of *Father* may be taken as a sign of their happiness in having their priests ministering to them. If the bishops may be regarded as the eyes that watch, the ears that listen, the tongue that speaks for the Church, priests may be regarded, under and with the bishops, as the hands that nourish the Mystical Body, as the feet that carry Christ's truth to all parts of the visible world.

The part that the laity plays in the Church is becoming constantly more important, as was proven by the discussion of the position of the laity in the apostolate of the Church in the Second Vatican Council. The members of the laity participate more and more directly in the work of spreading the Kingdom of the invisible Head. They also watch, listen and speak for the Church. They too are hands that minister to their fellow-members in Christ's body; they are feet that are tireless in going about, like their Master, doing good.

When we think of the proneness of human beings to disagree on every conceivable subject, particularly religion, the joy of the more than half-billion Catholics in the world on being united in belief, law and worship is not difficult to understand. "Gracious the sight, and full of comfort," sings the psalmist, "when brethren dwell united" (Ps. 132:1).

A member of the Church experiences a gladness that is hard to describe in the realization that he can enter a church in New York, or London, or Moscow, or Tokyo, or anywhere else on earth, and witness a visible verification of St. Paul's words: "You are one body, with a single Spirit; each of you, when he was called, called in the same hope; with the same Lord, the same faith, the same baptism; with the same God, the same Father, all of us, who is above all things, pervades all things, and lives in all of us" (Eph. 4:4-6).

Those who belong to Christ's Church never have to be concerned that they will hear a different doctrine preached from one country to another. A deep joy wells up within him, as a Catholic listens, wherever he goes, to the rolling cadences of the Nicene Creed: *I believe in one God, the Father Almighty, maker of heaven and earth, and of all things, visible and invisible. And in one Lord Jesus Christ, the only begotten Son of God, born of the Father before all ages; God of God, light of light, true God of true God. . . . Who for us men, and our salvation, came down from heaven; and was incarnate of the Virgin Mary; and was made man. . . . And in the Holy Spirit, the Lord and giver of life. . . . And one holy, catholic and apostolic Church. . . . And I await the resurrection of the dead, and the life of the world to come.*

The Church exults in the soul-stirring unity that marks her public worship of God. The same Mass is offered in some chapel hut in Africa as under the majestic dome of St. Peter's in Rome. There is never a moment of time when priests are not ascending altars to re-enact the Last Supper and Calvary's Sacrifice. As the earth rotates on its axis, and day begins in the different areas of the globe, the Mass also begins. Thus are fulfilled the words which God spoke ages ago through the prophet Malachias: "No corner of the world, from sun's rise to sun's setting, where the renown of me is not heard among the Gentiles, where sacrifice is not done, and pure offering made in my honor" (1:11).

Everywhere also there is the same pouring of water in baptism, the same imposition of the hand in confirmation, the same words of absolution in penance, the same living Bread in Communion, the same anointing in extreme unction, the same exchanging of vows in marriage, the same laying on of hands in holy orders.

When we consider the Church, we are looking at something which exists in this world, moves in this world, and uses the things of this world. But while the Church presents to the physical gaze of mankind a solid and impressive array of material buildings in which she gathers her members for worship, education, social action, recreation, medical care, she is in essence spiritual. This is evident from the very term we use to describe the Church. She is called the *Mystical Body of Christ.* This is the body of which St. Paul was writing when he said that we "have been baptized into a single body by the power of a single Spirit" (I Cor. 12:13).

The liturgy takes note of this twofold aspect of the Church when, in the postcommunion prayer of the Mass for the dedication of a church, she prays: *O God, who, out of living and chosen stones, dost prepare an eternal dwelling place for thy Majesty: help thy suppliant people: that as thy Church profits by material expansion, so may it also grow by spiritual increase. Through our Lord, Jesus Christ. . . .*

Realism demands that we recognize that any material expansion which is not accompanied with, or followed by, spiritual increase of some kind is an action that takes place strictly in the material order, without relevance to the spiritual nature of the Church. Those who act toward the Church as though she were just one more merely human organization do her the gravest disservice.

There are in the Church nominal members, those who "have been baptized into a single body," but who are outside the mainstream of supernatural life which flows through the Church "by the power of a single Spirit." Because they have forfeited authentic life in the Church, they have lost the joy of that life.

Since joy is consciousness of life, we can experience a joy in the Church such as the saints had only if we are living, as they did, in the full tide of her life. There is a deeply meaningful phrase which perfectly describes this idea of living by and with the Church: *sentire cum Ecclesia.* The phrase refers to that attitude toward the Church which is characterized by having one's whole personality, one's whole being, attuned to the Church. It means thinking, feeling, and acting with the Church.

Perhaps the best way for somebody outside the Church

to understand this total identification with the Church would be to go off somewhere and read biographies of saints, one after another. He would realize that not one of them could be understood except in the context of his life in the Church. He would see that the image of any saint he might analyze at random—St. Augustine, St. Benedict, St. Bernard, St. Thomas Aquinas, St. Ignatius, St. Vincent de Paul, St. Teresa, St. Frances Cabrini—would become distorted, and even grotesque, if torn from its proper place in the vast mosaic of Catholic life.

If the joy that the saints so obviously found in and through the Church is ever lacking in our lives, there is no need to be puzzled regarding the reason. It must be because our oneness with the Church has somehow been impaired. And this can happen in any one of four ways: by ceasing to think with the Church, or to feel with the Church, or to act with the Church, or to worship with the Church.

The total giving of oneself to the Church is marked by a joy that only the total giver can understand. In this giving there is no compulsion, unless we can talk of compulsion in regard to a completely convinced intellect, a completely captivated heart, a completely won will. The joy of the Church, in the last analysis, is the joy of integration. She integrates hundreds of thousands of persons of the most diverse races, nationalities, classes, in a body through which all these teeming members can find temporal and eternal fulfillment. Yet each retains complete individuality. Not only does he maintain his individuality, but through being integrated in the Church he develops an integrated personality. The saints are proof of this truth.

"Late have I loved thee, O Beauty so ancient and so

new," exclaimed St. Augustine to the Almighty, "late have I loved thee!" And he leaves no doubt where he had found God by saying, "the temple of God, that is, of the Holy Trinity as a whole, is the holy Church—everywhere, in heaven and on earth."

10. *The Joy of Truth*

"Do you know, my daughter, who they are that truly love me?" God asked St. Catherine of Siena. "They are those who recognize that whatever cannot be referred to me is falsehood." That truth is the core of everything that is good and beautiful is evident from the many references to truth in Holy Scripture. St. John says of Christ: "And the word was made flesh, and came to dwell among us; and we had sight of his glory, glory such as belongs to the Father's only-begotten Son, full of grace and truth" (Jn. 1:14). Our Lord said of himself: "I am truth and life" (Jn. 14:6). When he promised to send the Holy Spirit, he declared: "It will be for him, the truth-giving Spirit, when he comes, to guide you into all truth" (Jn. 16:13). He said that "true worshippers will worship the Father in spirit and in truth" (Jn. 4:23).

Because our joy in truth is all the deeper when we realize the evil of falsehood, it will be helpful to present evidence for the fact that falsehood is the fundamental evil, and that all other evils are rooted in it. That sage of the Far East, Confucius, indicated that to him falsehood meant the subversion of all order when, asked what he would do if requested to head a government, he replied: "Obviously, as a first step, I would see to it that things are called by their right names."

It is significant that the main title we give the devil is *Father of Lies.* He began his war against mankind by lying to Eve, and the essence of his strategy ever since has been deception. Going back beyond the world's creation, we find Satan bringing about his own damnation by lying to himself. "What, fallen from heaven, thou Lucifer," wrote Isaias, "that once didst herald the dawn? Prostrate on the earth, that didst once bring nations to their knees? I will scale the heavens (such was thy thought); I will set my throne higher than God's stars, take my seat at his own trysting-place . . . I will soar above the level of the clouds, the rival of the most High. Thine, instead, to be dragged down into the world beneath, into the heart of the abyss." (14:12-15) Christ said of this shattering result of the devil's self-deception: "I watched, while Satan was cast down like a lightning-flash from heaven" (Lk. 10:18).

That the generality of men have a consciousness of the evil of lying is shown by the profound feeling of insult that is experienced if one person says to another: *You are a liar.* This expression is far more deeply resented than the statement: *You lied.* The reason is obvious. When a man is called a liar, the person who calls him such is implying that his whole character is shot through with falsehood.

Every denial of true doctrine involves falsehood. Writing of the divinity of Christ, St. John asks: "To whom do we give the lie, if not to him who tells us that Jesus is not the Christ?" (I Jn. 2:22). The same can be said of anybody who denies the truth. Long before John, the psalmist said: "There is no God above us, is the fond thought of reckless hearts" (13:1). That is, of hearts reckless of the truth.

Moral evil is also rooted in lying. The proud, ascribing their talents to themselves, deny the divine Giver of the gifts they have received. They refuse to understand what St. Paul meant when he wrote: ". . . the man who plants, the man who waters, count for nothing. God is everything, since it is he who gives the increase." (I Cor. 3:7) The covetous man lies to himself when he says: *It is good for me to have this money, or this thing,* when what he covets belongs to somebody else.

The lustful man particularly appears to be conscious of lying to himself when he thinks: *It is good for me to indulge in this forbidden pleasure.* The glutton is guilty of self-deception when he says: *I cannot help this excessive eating or drinking; it is a compulsion beyond my control.* The envious person should know that he is deceiving himself when he thinks: *It is not good that my neighbor should have this good, which I lack.* The angry man lies to himself by saying: *This situation demands that I berate those concerned.* The sluggard, if he only gave it a moment's thought, would know that he is being false to God and to himself when he says: *It is not important that I exert myself.* In all these cases, the end is foretold by the author of Proverbs: "Never was a liar yet that escaped his doom" (19:5).

This may appear to be a roundabout way of leading up to joy in the truth, but there is no better way of appreciating light than to be plunged for a long time in darkness. When we consider the gloom which accompanies the darkness of falsehood, we become more aware of our joy in the light of truth. "False heart never found happiness," says the writer of Proverbs, "nor lying tongue escaped mischief" (17:20).

A good example of the melancholy results of falsehood is found in Communism. The earliest slogan of the Communists was a lie: *Workers of the world, unite. You have nothing to lose but your chains.* The gloom that has followed the application of the lying doctrine of Marxism hangs like a pall over the Communist countries. One of the most depressing sights on earth is the ugly, cruel Berlin wall. And one of the most melancholy events of our time was the ruthless suppression of the heroic Hungarian uprising. Instead of losing their chains, those who accepted the Communist lie lost their economic, political, social, intellectual and spiritual freedom.

Mankind has no liking for physical darkness, and this makes its descent into spiritual darkness all the sadder. Men are constantly using light to dispel darkness. We describe a cloudy day as a gloomy day. A beautiful day is one when the earth is bathed in sunlight. We describe a joyous person as a ray of sunshine. We speak of the sunny side of life.

The light that is so frequently mentioned in Holy Scripture is the light of God's truth. Christ, who said "I am truth," was referring to this attribute in himself when he declared: "I am the light of the world. He who follows me can never walk in darkness; he will possess the light which is life." (Jn. 8:12) In the sublime prose poem with which St. John starts his Gospel, the phrases leap with light: ". . . and God had the Word abiding with him, and the Word was God. . . . In him there was life, and that life was the light of men. And the light shines in darkness, a darkness which was not able to master it. . . . There is one who enlightens every soul born into the world; he was the true Light." (Jn. 1:1-10)

After John had begun to preach Christ as Truth incarnate, he continued to express the truth in terms of light.

Referring to our Lord, he wrote: "The true light is now shining" (I Jn. 2:8, CV). In words that glow with beauty and joy, St. Paul seems to be unable to contain his gladness in having the darkness of his early errors dispelled by Christ's truth. He writes to the Corinthians: "The same God who bade light shine out of darkness has kindled a light in our hearts, whose shining is to make known his glory as he has revealed it in the features of Jesus Christ" (II Cor. 4:6).

Men's instinctive search for truth in the natural order, and their satisfaction in finding it, is revealed in various phrases that are always on their lips. They are satisfied only when they have *true weight, true measure, true proportion, true color, true tone.* They are not happy unless they feel that they have received *a true estimate, a true report, a true picture.*

That truth is generally respected is shown by the fact that no quality in another person is more valued than veracity. Whether you are dealing with husband, wife, employer, employee, seller, buyer, doctor or lawyer, nothing gives greater satisfaction than the conviction that the person you are dealing with is truthful. When a child has misbehaved, the parent will show his innate love for truth by saying: *I will forgive you, if you will only tell the truth.* God's pleasure in seeing his truth reflected in us is indicated in the words he spoke through Zacharias: It "shall be all rejoicing and gladness. . . . all high festival, will you but love true dealing and peaceful ways" (8:19).

There is a radiance that shines from the face and eyes of the person who loves the truth. People sense this quality in the man who possesses it, and they rejoice in it, even if they do not understand or analyze their joy in such a person's presence.

Man's highest faculty is his mind, and the mind is satisfied when it comes into possession of its proper object, which is truth. "Prize of the discerning heart, quest of the wise man's ear," says the Book of Proverbs, "is to learn truth" (18:15).

Freedom of mind and heart is an indispensable condition for true joy. That freedom is an effect of truth is made clear by Christ's words: "You will come to know the truth, and the truth will set you free" (Jn. 8:32). The truthful person is set free from falsehood, and from all the evil that flows from it. He is free to enjoy the light of truth in this world, so often afflicted with physical and spiritual darkness. He will be free to enjoy the Vision of God in heaven, where his mind will see light in him who is Light, truth in him who is Truth.

11. *The Joy of Wisdom*

There is an awesome passage in the Prophecy of Jeremias which will find terrifying fulfillment in an atomically devastated world if a greater proportion of men do not open their eyes to the beauty and joy of true wisdom. "Earthward I looked, and all was void and empty; heavenward, and in heaven no light shone; looked at mountain and hillside, and saw them stir and tremble; looked for some sign of man, and in vain; the very birds of heaven had all taken flight. It was a garden I looked at, but a garden untenanted; no city in it but had perished at the Lord's glance, before the frown of his vengeance." (Jer. 4:23-26)

Self-deception often makes man unable to see the distinction between worldly intelligence and spiritual wisdom. The wonderful works of man in the physical order are overpowering. One sees human beings walking past a towering skyscraper, and they appear incredibly dwarfed. And yet it was such comparatively tiny beings who shot that mass of steel and concrete skyward. Or one watches people crossing a bridge of heroic proportions, looking like the six-inch inhabitants of Lilliput. And yet it was these seemingly microscopic creatures who threw that structure, with all its strength and grace, from shore to shore. The magnificent physical works of man are the result of his knowledge, skill and industry. Although these qualities are gifts that man has received from God, they are of the natural order.

Any person who pauses to consider the matter cannot fail to realize the joy that would come to mankind were man's natural knowledge, skill and industry accompanied by divine wisdom. Then man would build in his soul a spiritual structure that would finally reach into heaven itself. He would apply to himself with joy words written by St. Paul: "You. . . are a structure of God's design. . . . I have laid a foundation as a careful architect should. . . . The foundation which has been laid is the only one which anybody can lay: I mean Jesus Christ." (I Cor. 3:9-11) Scripture does more than speak of the wisdom of Christ. It calls him *"the wisdom of God"* (I Cor. 1:24). Once a man has the wisdom to make Christ his foundation, he continues to need the wisdom of Christ if he is to build on Christ. He must understand with the psalmist that "vain is the builder's toil, if the house is not of the Lord's building" (Ps. 126:1).

The joy of mankind would be increased incalculably if man's skill in building bridges in the material world were only matched by wisdom to build bridges in the spiritual order. Christ is called *Pontifex,* which means bridge-builder. He built a bridge between God and man, between heaven and earth. It is his will that we imitate his wisdom by helping to build bridges between man and man, between the nations of man, between the races of man. John Donne was not entirely accurate when he said that *no man is an island.* Any man who unwisely cuts himself off from God or his fellowman, or from both, becomes an island, joyless and desolate.

In order to highlight the joy of spiritual wisdom, we have to return to a consideration of the foolhardiness that marks the lives of those who reject divine wisdom. God addresses the spiritually foolish through Jeremias: "Ah, reckless people of mine, that would not acknowledge me; blind fools, for mischief so shrewd, in well-doing so untutored!" (Jer. 4:22). Satan was the first fool in the spiritual order, and the only satisfaction left to him is to make fools of human beings. How well he succeeds is evident when one tallies the various meanings of the verb, *to fool.* It means: *to treat with contempt; to disappoint; to defeat; to frustrate; to deceive; to impose upon.* Other meanings are: *to infatuate; to make foolish.* And, finally, it means: *to cheat.* Anybody with self-respect feels insulted, mortified and angered if he is made a fool of in any of the senses mentioned. Unfortunately, this is true of most people only with regard to worldly matters. The devil can treat them with utter contempt, disappoint, defeat, frustrate, deceive and cheat them, in the spiritual order, and they do not even realize what is going on.

The graphic phrase, "for mischief so shrewd," which

God put in the mouth of Jeremias, describes perfectly the worldly wisdom of those who bring such grief to their fellowmen in this world, and to themselves in eternity. They are intelligent, without being wise. They have an evil shrewdness but are destitute of spiritual wisdom. Their malicious cunning sometimes amounts to diabolical genius. Illustrations of this are found in all strata of society, from the malevolent craftiness of the leaders of world Communism to the impish sleight of hand of an expert pickpocket.

Writing about worldly wisdom, the spiritually wise genius St. Thomas Aquinas says: "Whoever turns away from his rightful end must of necessity fix on some unrightful end, since every agent acts for an end. Wherefore, if he fixes his end in external, earthly things, his *wisdom* is called *earthly;* if in bodily goods, it is called *sensual wisdom;* if in some spiritual excellence, it is called *devilish wisdom,* since it imitates the devil's pride, of which it is written: 'Over all the pride of earth he reigns supreme' " (Job. 41:25). Worldly wisdom may be said to be Satan's gift to spiritual fools.

Spiritual wisdom is the gift of God's Spirit, and from this wisdom flows in a particular way that joy which Scripture calls one of the fruits of the Holy Spirit. It will be helpful to recall the way in which the joy of faith and the joy of wisdom are linked. Through faith, we have the joy of looking into the unseen world, and of perceiving the splendid realities of that world. Through the gift of wisdom, we have the joy of judging all things according to the realities of the invisible world.

Wisdom gives us the joy of judging everything according to the mind of God himself. Through the gift of wisdom, God lets us into his secrets. St. Paul shows how this is accomplished by the Spirit of God, who dwells in us:

"What we make known is the wisdom of God, his secret. . . . So we read of, Things no eye has seen, no ear has heard, no human heart conceived, the welcome God has prepared for those who love him. To us, then, God has made a revelation of it through his Spirit; there is no depth in God's nature so deep that the Spirit cannot find it out. Who else can know a man's thoughts, except the man's own spirit that is within him? So no one else can know God's thoughts, but the Spirit of God. . . . Mere man with his natural gifts cannot take in the thoughts of God's Spirit; they seem mere folly to him, and he cannot grasp them, because they demand a scrutiny which is spiritual. Whereas the man who has spiritual gifts can scrutinize everything. . . ." (I Cor. 2:7-16)

It was of Christ, Incarnate Wisdom, that Isaias said: "One shall be born, on whom the spirit of the Lord will rest; a spirit wise and discerning . . ." (Is. 11:2). During his earthly life, wisdom flowed from his lips. His listeners were overcome with admiration for a wisdom such as no other man had ever manifested. St. Matthew says that even his enemies were "full of admiration at his words" (Matt. 22:22).

After two thousand years, there is still inexhaustible joy in contemplating the wisdom that causes the pages of the Gospels to glow with a divine light. There is unique satisfaction in observing the wisdom with which Jesus confronted the world as he found it. He saw evils that may have been worse than those we see today. His scathing condemnation of the scribes and Pharisees reveals only one aspect of the evil with which he had to contend. He was aware of the venality of Pilate, by whom he would be unjustly condemned to death. He knew the corruption of the Jewish priests, who would not rest until they had his crucified and entombed body placed safely, as they foolishly supposed, under a military guard. He saw the greed of the money changers in the precincts of the Temple, his Father's house.

All these evils flowed out to impede his divine mission. With serene wisdom, he met them head on, and conquered them. In him there was neither the compromise of those who remain silent, to safeguard their worldly interests, nor the defeatism of those who succumb to world-weariness. It would have been so easy for him to have stopped talking about the terrible evils that surrounded him. If he had suddenly ceased condemning, he could have escaped crucifixion.

Fools that they were, his enemies were always trying to "put him to the test," as when the Pharisees and Sadducees asked him to show them a sign from heaven. It is not difficult to picture these men talking together before they approached our Lord. They probably exchanged feeble jokes as they walked up to him, and asked that he give them a sign. He was ready for them, and thwarted their childish plans to entrap him. He told them that they could read the skies, morning and evening, to determine the weather, as could any bright child, but could "not read the signs of appointed times." It was on this occasion that he hinted about his resurrection by referring to the sign of Jonas, who had been in the whale's belly three days and nights, saying that this was the only sign that would be given to "a wicked and unfaithful generation that asks for a sign." (Matt. 16:1-4) And when this sign was fulfilled by his rising from the dead, his enemies continued to make fools of themselves. St. Matthew says that they "offered a rich bribe to the soldiers. Let this, they said, be your tale, His disciples came by night and stole him away, while we were asleep" (Matt. 28:12, 13).

As St. Augustine says, the unwise love of money which

had taken captive one of Christ's companions, a disciple, also took captive the military guard at the tomb. The great doctor of the Church pours scorn on the worldly wisdom displayed by the Pharisees and Sadducees on this occasion. It was a perfect example of the way in which the wisdom of worldlings so frequently defeats itself. "O unhappy cunning," comments St. Augustine, "did you so far forsake godly wisdom and plunge yourself so deep in craftiness as . . . to bring forward witnesses who were asleep? Truly you yourselves must have fallen asleep, thus to defeat your own purpose."

His enemies never seemed to learn from their constant defeats not to engage in a battle of wits with the wisest of men. With unbounded admiration, we watch as he defeats their chicanery, time after time, often with one declarative sentence. Those who love true wisdom experience a thrill of joy in witnessing an intellectual duel in which a spiritually wise man brilliantly worsts a satanically cunning adversary.

They were forever trying to impale him on the horns of a dilemma, and forever walking away defeated. Once they thought to involve him in politics by asking whether it was right to pay the tax imposed by their Roman conquerors. His was a purely spiritual mission, and to become involved in political disputes would have hindered the work he had come to accomplish. He asked to be shown the coin with which the tax was paid. When they had brought him a silver piece, he asked whose name and image it bore. When they replied that the image and inscription were Caesar's, he answered with a wisdom that astounded them: "Why then, give back to Caesar what is Caesar's, and to God what is God's" (Matt. 22:21). The Gospel says that "they went away and left him in peace, full of admiration at his words" (22:22).

At another time, they brought before him a woman who had been caught in the act of adultery. They reminded him that the law of Moses ordered death by stoning as punishment for adultery, and then they asked what sentence he would pass on the fallen woman. If he answered that he would forgive her, they were ready to accuse him of opposing the law. If, on the other hand, he ordered her to be stoned, they knew that those standing around would accuse him of being merciless.

He tried to save these evil men public embarrassment by writing on the ground, but they refused to accept his tactful silence. When they persisted with the question, looking into their evil hearts and faces, he said: "Whichever of you is free from sin shall cast the first stone at her." With a considerateness that they did not deserve, he again bent down and started writing on the ground. St. John says that "they began to go out one by one, beginning with the eldest." (Jn. 8:3-9)

There is undoubtedly great excitement in watching the machinations of people who are evil geniuses. This explains why the preponderance of successful plays, motion pictures and television programs are about the activities of men and women who fascinate the viewer by their worldly cunning. It is not surprising that *fascination* has its root in the Latin verb meaning *to bewitch.* Those who have the faculty of judging wisely recognize the difference between the beguilement that may result from a display of worldly cunning and the authentic joy that results from a manifestation of genuine wisdom. They understand with the author of the Book of Wisdom that "never yet did wisdom find her way into the schemer's heart, never yet made her home in a life mortgaged to sin" (Wis. 1:4). In *Murder in the Cathedral,* by T. S.

Eliot, the spectator may be intrigued by the craftiness of King Henry and his courtiers, but he is charmed by the wisdom of St. Thomas Becket.

The long and noble line of saints, who raised mankind's sights to the highest heavens, illustrate the power and joy that spring from the application of the wisdom of Christ to everyday life. That their wisdom came from the Spirit of God is demonstrated by the fact that it is found, not only in men of towering intellect like St. Augustine and St. Thomas, but in unlettered children like St. Bernadette. When learned theologians tried to trap her into making statements which would cast doubt on the authenticity of the apparitions of our Lady that she claimed to have had, she answered their questions with a wisdom that could not have been other than supernatural. They asked her, for example, whether she was happier when she had the apparitions, or when she received her first Communion, a question calculated to perplex and disconcert even a well-informed and alert adult. She replied, in effect, that there was no need to compare the joy of these occasions because they complemented one another.

We see reflected in the saints, as in so many mirrors, the wisdom of Christ, their Master. They prove to mankind that men universally would become a race of sages if they were to weigh and apply the golden words garnered by the writers of the Gospels. They make us understand that the wisdom contained in the Sermon on the Mount, comprising only three of the twenty-eight chapters of St. Matthew's Gospel, if generally applied, would so change the tired world that we would hardly recognize it.

Our joy in Christ's wisdom is naturally increased by the beauty of phrase with which he clothed it. He does not just tell us to manifest wisdom by having absolute confidence in the all-embracing and all-loving care of our Father in heaven. He says: "See how the birds of the air never sow, or reap, or gather grain into barns, and yet your heavenly Father feeds them; have you not an excellence beyond theirs? . . . And why should you be anxious over clothing? See how the wild lilies grow; they do not toil or spin; and yet I tell you that even Solomon in all his glory was not arrayed like one of these. If God, then, so clothes the grasses of the field, which today live and will feed the oven tomorrow, will he not be much more ready to clothe you, men of little faith?" (Matt. 6:25-30) When a member of the British Parliament used this lovely passage in a speech, one of his colleagues, unbelievably unaware of its source, complimented him on the extraordinary gracefulness of his expression.

When he warns us of the folly of becoming so absorbed in the things of this world that we forget those of eternity, he again presents his wise counsel in compelling metaphor: "Do not lay up treasure for yourselves on earth, where there is rust and moth to consume it, where there are thieves to break in and steal it; lay up treasure for yourselves in heaven, where there is no moth or rust to consume it, no thieves to break in and steal" (Matt. 6:19, 20).

In telling us not to be so unwise as to spoil our good works through vainglory, he puts his wise advice in one graphic sentence: ". . . thou shalt not so much as let thy left hand know what thy right hand is doing" (Matt. 6:3).

To those who unwisely go out to meet trouble before it arrives, he says: "Do not fret over tomorrow; leave tomorrow to fret over its own needs; for today, today's troubles are enough" (Matt. 6:34). The wisdom of this counsel is more evident when we consider the unnecessary sorrow that people bring into their lives by worrying about the future. Our Lord does not say that troubles do not await us. What he is saying is that we aggravate them by piling future difficulties, some of which may not even materialize, on the difficulties of the present. Wisdom makes us realize that we have only the present day, the present hour, and that the past is over forever, the future in the hands of God.

Still again, Christ indicates the lack of wisdom shown by a man who would sit in judgment on his fellowman, while his own vices or shortcomings are more obvious than those of the man he is so eager to judge. In a few telling phrases, he draws a picture of the person who is blind to his own faults, but sees so clearly the faults of those around him. Our Lord puts it this way: "By what right wilt thou say to thy brother, Wait, let me rid thy eye of that speck, when all the while there is a beam in thy own? Thou hypocrite, take the beam out of thy own eye, and so thou shalt have clear sight to rid thy brother's of the speck." (Matt. 7:4, 5)

And when it comes to urging us to set an example for others by letting his light shine through us, he uses another striking analogy: "A lamp is not lighted to be put away under a bushel measure; it is put on the lampstand, to give light to all the people of the house; and your light must shine so brightly before men that they can see your good works, and glorify your Father who is in heaven" (Matt. 5:15, 16).

One of the signs of a truly wise man is the acknowledgment that he has failed often to live according to the wisdom that Christ has so lavishly bestowed upon his Church. We all make mistakes, but it is only the wise who are willing to recognize the wrong turns that they have taken. As the writer of Ecclesiasticus says: "Only the wise man knows the slips of his own heart" (Ecclus. 21:8). God says to all of his sons: "Must I ever be offering thee sonship, and a land so fair that all the peoples of the world might envy thee its possession? Must I ever be pleading with thee to acknowledge me as thy father, and forsake my guidance no more?" (Jer. 3:19) And again, he reasons with us: "Would you grudge free expense of silver in the search for wisdom, that shall make you ample returns in gold?" (Ecclus. 51:36).

12. *The Joy of Peace*

The joy that springs from peace would be appreciated more if the meaning of peace itself were better understood. It is a disservice to the concept of peace to think of it as merely a lack of disturbance. Peace is far from being a negative quality. That it is, on the contrary, a positive quality becomes evident from the classic definition of peace given by St. Augustine. He says that peace is the *tranquility of order.*

Perhaps the greatest visible manifestation of order is the precise movement of the billions of stars and planets through space. We are both awed and reassured by the order with which the Creator has arranged the motion of the heavenly bodies. We talk about peaceful weather, or a peaceful sea, not because there is no weather, nor sea, but because the elements constituting them are *in order.*

It is true that joy is found in that absence of disturbance which is the negative aspect of peace. The explosive joy that followed the signing of the armistice ending World War I was so great that it was memorialized through the establishment of a national holiday. But even in a case like this, the joy is based, not merely on the cessation of warfare, but the return of fighting men to the positive order of peaceful civil life. Isaias was referring to the positive aspect of peace when he said that when peace came, men would not just destroy their swords and spears, but that "they will melt their swords into plowshares, their spears into pruning hooks" (Is. 2:4). He does not present us with a picture of men laying down their arms and then sitting around, frittering away their time. The picture he draws is of men in the fields, engaged in healthful and fruitful pursuits in an atmosphere of peace.

The cause of religion is hardly served by those who give the impression that religious peace is something dull and joyless. Energetic spirits are naturally repelled by a peace whose main characteristic appears to be boredom. Those who love life and action cannot be blamed if they are adversely affected by the unfortunate and silly idea of heaven as a place where the saints stand around forever singing psalms. The God who created life and energy in its manifold forms would hardly inhabit a heaven marked by such dullness. He who fashioned man's body for action would not ask him to settle down in his glorified state to an eternity of inaction.

The peace which Christ brought to those to whom he ministered during those three years which are called his public life was the *tranquility of order*. He, the personification of that eternal peace which is nothing else than eternal order, brought the tranquility of order into the minds and hearts of those who opened their souls to him.

That this peace was not a form of inaction is evident from the example of action which he gave his disciples.

The caricatures of him which so many of his modern followers circulate, showing an effete, posturing figure, insult him. They do not represent him, but misrepresent him. His serene contemplation of the Godhead did not prevent his being a Man of action. The peace which he came to bring was not only compatible with strenuous activity but manifested itself in such activity.

Being peaceable does not mean being passionless. Virtues are passions in order, while vices are passions in disorder. The saints could not by any means be described as men and women without passion. We have only to mention men like Moses, Abraham, David, John the Baptist, Simon Peter, Saul of Tarsus, the Sons of Thunder, Leo the Great, Benedict of Nursia, Gregory the Great, Patrick, Bernard, Francis of Assisi, Ignatius Loyola, Vincent de Paul, Thomas More, to demonstrate that the peace that goes with sanctity is a positive quality, and one entirely compatible with strenuous action. This idea is confirmed when we consider women who have achieved heroic sanctity. Nobody would regard as lacking a certain desirable aggressiveness such Old Testament heroines as Sarah, Rebecca, Ruth, Judith and Esther—the last three having been such women of action that Old Testament Books are named for them. We find in them all that blend of peacefulness and action that adds to the attractiveness of spiritual peace. It is discovered again in the Mother of the Lord, and in the other women who were obviously such a source of encouragement to him in his ministry. It is found in such towering personalities as Monica, Catherine of Siena, Joan of Arc, Jane Frances de Chantal, Teresa of Avila, Elizabeth Seton, Frances Cabrini.

That Pope John XXIII made a unique contribution to

the joy of those who were privileged to live during his brief reign was evident from the expression of regret on the part of so many outside the Church, as well as within, when he died. It is significant that this man of overflowing peace should have written, as one of his last acts, an encyclical, *Peace on Earth,* which has been hailed by both Catholics and non-Catholics as a blueprint for order in men, nations and the world. He said that outside our Father in heaven, outside his wisdom, his will, his rule, there was nothing but discord.

The joy that walks hand in hand with peace spreads from the individual whose soul is at peace to his family, then to his community, then to his nation, and finally to the world. Peace, like war, has its beginning, as far as this world is concerned, in the human heart. Of course, it ultimately comes from God, from whom all order proceeds. If there are enough people on earth who have peace in their hearts, there will be peace on earth, just as there is bound to be external warfare if there are enough men and women in the world who are at war within themselves. Both peace and warfare are an externalization of the peace and warfare in men's souls.

The likelihood of peace in the world increases in proportion to the order that exists in human minds, hearts and consciences. Everybody wants peace on earth, but not everybody is willing to make his contribution to that peace by establishing order in his own life. Everybody wants the joy of peace, but not everybody is willing to do what is necessary to ensure peace.

Men often talk about peace of mind, but not many understand that peace in the mind is the result of order in the mind. And order in the mind is the effect of truth in the mind. When a person's mind is divorced from truth, his mind is sick. What is not generally recognized is that true peace of mind begins with a recognition of the truth about one's relationship to the universe and its Creator. This must be followed by an understanding of the truth regarding one's actual relationship to others. And this, naturally, depends on seeing the truth about one's spiritual state.

Peace of heart depends on the order that exists in one's will. The heart is a symbol of the will. It is possible for a person to possess truth in his mind, and yet have a heart completely divided from God because of rebellion against his will. This attitude of heart is referred to by Isaias when he says: "For the rebellious, the Lord says, there is no peace" (Is. 57:21). If peace of mind is combined with peace of heart, a man's spiritual house is in perfect order. The joy of soul that results from such harmony has to be experienced to be described. "Very great peace is theirs who love thy law," sings the psalmist; "their feet never stumble" (Ps. 118:165). Such a peace is the gift of the Prince of Peace, as he indicated when he said to the disciples at the Last Supper: "Peace is my bequest to you, and the peace which I will give you is mine to give" (Jn. 14:27).

Scripture gives expression to the temptation that comes to the just man on seeing the apparent peace of those who disobey God's law: "Yet I was near losing my foothold, felt the ground sink under my steps, such heart-burning had I at seeing the good fortune of sinners that defy his law" (Ps. 72:2-3). Professedly atheistic dictators often appear to enjoy an enviable peace. But this peace Christ rejected when he promised his peace to the Apostles: "I do not give peace as the world gives it" (Jn. 14:27).

The peace that the world gives is a counterfeit peace because it is based on self-deception. Things are not as the atheist pretends they are. One day his world of lies will collapse, just as the castle that the child labors so hard to build in the sand is washed away by a sudden wave. Such self-deception is seen in a member of the Church who seeks peace, and the joy of it, in a life of sin. Frequently panic can be detected in such a person's response to a friend who tries to awaken him from his false sense of peace. The one involved is liable to say heatedly that he does not want to discuss the matter. While this could be the result of resentment at another's intrusion into his personal affairs, the abruptness of manner gives the impression that the outburst is due to a fear that further discussion will expose the false peace and happiness for what they are.

Those who sink into the illusory peace that accompanies surrender to evil passion do not want to be reminded of the authentic peace that is the reward of overcoming passion. They have surrendered the citadel of their souls, and they have no taste for the battle that would be involved in winning it back. We are confronted here with the paradox that we cannot enjoy spiritual peace without a constant struggle. The peace of which the angels sang at Bethlehem, the peace which Christ gave to his disciples, is a peace which can be won only by those who are willing to fight.

Before Job regained the peace which surrounded his early life, he had to pass through such combat that he lamented: "What is man's life on earth but a compaigning? Like a hired drudge, he passes his time away; nor ever was slave so weary, longing for the shade, or drudge so weary, waiting to earn his hire, as I have been, counting these months of emptiness, these nights that never brought rest." (Job 7:1-3) This sounds like a contradiction of peace, but all the while Job was engaged in dire struggle, his mind and heart were being molded by the God of peace. That peace which is the result of spiritual order began to return to his soul little by little, until Scripture shows him, in the end, a figure of serenity.

The peace that existed in the mind and heart of St. Paul can be judged by the order that his words have brought into the lives of countless Christians down the ages. However, in him we have another outstanding example of the connection between peace and struggle. "Inwardly, I applaud God's disposition," he writes to the Romans, "but I observe another disposition in my lower self, which raises war against the disposition of my conscience . . ." (Rom. 7:22-23). This Paul, whose epistles contain so many references to peace, wrote to Timothy: "Fight the good fight of the faith, lay thy grasp on eternal life . . ." (I Tim. 6:12). And the Epistle to the Hebrews, with its great air of serene contemplation of eternal verities, calls its recipients to combat with these challenging words: "Why then, since we are watched from above by such a cloud of witnesses, let us rid ourselves of all that weighs us down, of the sinful habit that clings so closely, and run, with all endurance, the race for which we are entered. Let us fix our eyes on Jesus, the origin and the crown of all faith, who, to win his prize of blessedness, endured the cross and made light of its shame, Jesus, who now sits at the right of God's throne." (Heb. 12:1-2)

The joy that springs from spiritual peace is a secure joy. It is not affected by the most adverse external circumstances. While St. Augustine was bishop of Hippo in northern Africa, there was an invasion of that area by Vandals from Europe. During the invasion, he began a sermon with a text on peace. No sooner had the word peace fallen from his lips than there was an audible sigh from the congregation. The people were thinking of the peace that would follow the withdrawal of the barbarians from their country. St. Augustine went on to show them that they could enjoy a very real peace even during the invasion, namely, peace of soul. St. Thomas More enjoyed such a deep spiritual peace that he could make a witty remark moments before his head fell from the headman's block.

St. Thomas Aquinas links the beatitude *Blessed are the peacemakers* with the supreme gift of the Holy Spirit, that of wisdom. Wisdom causes its possessor to rise above the world and to see all human events from the viewpoint of God and eternity. There are many events in human life, from a buzzing mosquito to the outbreak of war, which are capable of disturbing our peace. Statistics gathered in the United States during a recent year showed that more than two hundred thousand persons had found life's annoyances so great that they attempted to escape them through suicide. The person who has peace of soul fits the most disturbing incidents and events into the pattern that God has given mankind in his Scriptures.

Paraphrasing his word, we can say that all things work together for *peace* in those who love God (Rom. 8:28). When St. Thomas says that *peace is the perfection of joy,* he explains that peace removes those external disturbances which, if not controlled by our minds and wills, would interfere with our enjoyment of union with God. Spiritual joy also depends on peace to quiet, or keep in order, those interior desires which, if they became rampant, would destroy our peace and our joy.

It is obvious that a great deal of self-discipline is involved in the attainment of the joy that comes with peace.

Holy Scripture again explains the sequence: "For the time being, all correction is painful rather than pleasant; but afterwards, when it has done its work of discipline, it yields a harvest of good dispositions, to our great peace" (Heb. 12:11).

The real joy in the peace that is ours during this earthly pilgrimage is only a foretaste of the joy that will be ours when we enter that eternal peace which awaits us in the eternal kingdom of the Prince of Peace.

13. The Joy of the Cross

In the midst of the somber liturgy of the Friday of the Passion and Death of the Lord, with the ministers of the service wearing the black vestments of mourning, the Church suddenly strikes a high note of exultation: *for behold! by the wood of the Cross joy came into the whole world.* Immediately after this antiphon, in the hymn, *Faithful Cross,* we are singing of the Cross in such joyful phrases as *O tree of beauty, noble tree, tree divine.* Thus we are reminded that all the joy we possess through membership in the Church, as well as the joy that will be ours in heaven, has come to us from the Cross.

It would be a tragic mistake to forget the sorrowful aspects of the Passion and Cross of our divine Redeemer. Very seldom is the figure of our Lord on the cross which is used at Mass clothed in the vestments of priesthood. He is the supreme Priest, the great High Priest, offering himself in sacrifice, but the Church does not want us to forget what his sacrifice cost him.

There is no more joyful service in the liturgy than the Easter Vigil, which heralds the glorious resurrection of our Savior. But various parts of the ceremonies remind us that our Easter joy flows from the Cross. The priest cuts the sign of the cross into the Easter candle, and while doing so says: *Christ, yesterday and today, the beginning and the end.* He then cuts the first letter of the Greek alphabet above the cross, and the last letter under it, recalling the words of the Apocalypse: "I am Alpha, I am Omega, the beginning of all things and their end, says the Lord" (1:8). Inscribing the current year above and under the arms of the cross, the priest says: *His are the seasons, his the ages. To him be glory and dominion through ages eternal.*

Stressing the connection between the Cross and our Lord's resurrection, the priest inserts grains of incense imbedded in red wax in the form of nails in the center and four points of the cross. He accompanies this action with the words: *By his wounds, holy and glorious, may he protect us and preserve us, who is Christ the Lord.* Because the great Easter candle represents the risen Lord, the priest says, as he lights it, *Christ rises resplendent.*

These are the wounds that Jesus showed to the doubting Thomas after the resurrection. With divine condescension, he said: "Let me have thy finger; see, here are my hands. Let me have thy hand; put it into my side. Cease thy doubting, and believe." Thomas could only reply: "Thou art my Lord and my God." (Jn. 20:27-28)

When we think of his Cross, meditating on his most bitter agony, it is a joy to know that the grievous wounds made by the nails and the spear now shine resplendently in heaven. As St. Ambrose wrote, "Our Lord desired to bring to heaven the wounds he had accepted in our behalf. These he was unwilling to relinquish, that he might show them to God the Father as the price of our liberty."

Our joy in the Cross is expressed with great beauty in that masterpiece of music and literature, the *Exsultet,* sung during the Easter Vigil. "O incomprehensible goodness of love," the Church sings; "to redeem a slave thou didst deliver up a Son! O truly necessary sin of Adam, which the death of Christ has blotted out! O happy fault, that merited a Redeemer so holy and so great!"

It was not by chance that St. John said that the lance which was thrust into the side and heart of the dead Lord on the Cross *opened,* instead of pierced, his side. We all share the joy of St. Augustine when he writes: "Christ is the Gate, and this same Gate was opened to you when the lance pierced his side. . . . It was for me that Longinus opened the side of Jesus with his lance, and so I enter there, and there I rest full of security. Therefore let him who fears, now love, for love casts out fear."

The same joy is shown by St. John Chrysostom when he exults: "One of the soldiers pierced the side of Jesus, and opened for us the way into the sacred Temple. It is there that I have found my bright treasure, and there that I rejoice to find all gleaming riches." St. Anselm joins the chorus of joy by exclaiming: "This pierced side of Christ is the wound that has given us a glimpse into the treasure-trove of his goodness, that is to say the love of his heart for us." St. Bernard manifests his delight in contemplating Christ's open side and heart when he writes: "I have found the heart of my King and my Brother, and that of my loving Friend Jesus. What more can I desire in heaven, or what more seek upon the earth?"

Our Lord himself explained to St. Catherine of Siena why he had allowed his side to be opened on the Cross.

"My purpose," he told her, "was to discover to men the secret of my heart, so that they might know that my love is greater than the external signs I give of it. For while there was an end to my sufferings, my love for men is without limit."

Men and women hunger for love, and here they have God literally opening his heart to them. The love manifested by Christ on the Cross is a perfect fulfillment of the words God spoke through Jeremias: "With unchanging love I love thee, and now in mercy I have drawn thee to myself" (31:3). And words that he uttered through Osee could have been on the lips of the Divine Redeemer on the Cross: "Yet it was I, none other, guided those first steps of theirs, and took them in my arms, and healed, all unobserved, their injuries. Sons of Adam, they should be drawn with leading strings of love." (11:3-4)

"This is the greatest love a man can show," our Lord said, "that he should lay down his life for his friends" (Jn. 15:13). We must all feel unworthy of such a love as his. But we can take encouragement in that the first person to receive an external manifestation of Christ's love from the Cross was Dismas, a sinner like us. We can all experience a joy similar to that of the man we now call the Good Thief in the truth that the love which the Lord gave to him he also gives to us.

The exchange between Christ and the thief is like a ray of light piercing the gloom hanging over Calvary. That the man had been a great sinner is apparent in his telling the thief on the other cross that their punishment fitted their crimes. Nobody would say that he was being treated justly if, for petty theft, he had to submit to the most brutal form of execution probably ever devised. That the Gospel states he was a thief is no indication that he was not more than that. Perceiving the divine in spite of all the shame and humiliation of the cross, he calls Jesus *Lord*. "Lord," he says, "remember me when thou comest into thy Kingdom." In spite of his indescribable torment, his heart must have been pounding with joy as he heard the reply: "I promise thee, this day thou shalt be with me in Paradise." (Lk. 23:42-43)

Good Friday has been called the saddest and gladdest of days. We cannot fail to experience a very great sadness in gazing on the blood-stained, sweat-stained face of the most beautiful of the sons of men. We feel profound sorrow at the torture caused him by the thorns and nails, by the agonizing posture in which he is held, by his difficulty in breathing, by his awful thirst. It would be inhuman not to be moved by such intolerable pain. But entwined with this sadness is our gladness that what he endures proves beyond all doubt that we are loved by him whose love ultimately is the only one that really matters.

We have joy in the Cross because through it a Man who is also God gave his life for us, and to us. He gave his mortal life for us that we might be saved from eternal misery. He gave his divine life to us to prepare us for a participation in the peace, joy and glory of his heavenly Kingdom. All our joy in believing, hoping and loving proceeds from the Cross. Our joy in being members of his Mystical Body, sons of God, temples of his Spirit, also comes from the Cross. Our joy in repenting if we have wandered away from him, in having his sacrifice continued on our altars, in having him come to us in Holy Communion, in having his Mother as ours, likewise is ours because of his Cross.

The popes of our time, when devotion to Christ's Sacred Heart has become so widespread, have expressed themselves with what might almost be called rapture in writing about the heart that was opened for us on the Cross. Pope Leo XIII, who dedicated the world to the Sacred Heart during the Holy Year he decreed for opening the present century, wrote in an encyclical marking the event: "Behold another most auspicious and divine standard presented to our view today: the Most Sacred Heart of Jesus, gleaming with dazzling light, surrounded by flames. In it all our hopes must be placed, in it man's salvation must be sought and looked for."

Pope St. Pius X, in his encyclical on the Sacred Heart, wrote with a like fervor: "Is not the epitome of religion, and, consequently, the norm of the more perfect life, contained in that form of piety which more readily leads souls to acknowledge Christ the Lord, and which more effectively inclines hearts to love him more ardently, and imitate him more closely?"

Joining their predecessors in hymning the praises of the heart that gave its last drop of blood for us on the Cross, Popes Pius XI and XII wrote encyclical letters on the Divine Heart. Pius XII wrote: "The Heart of Christ is the clearest image of the fullness of God embracing all things. By this, we mean the fullness of mercy, which is the special characteristic of the New Testament, in which 'the goodness and kindness of God, our Savior, appeared.' " Referring to devotion to our Lord's Sacred Heart, he says in another place: "What act of religion is nobler, more suitable, sweeter, and more conducive to salvation, since this devotion is wholly directed to the love of God himself?"

When we raise our eyes to the Cross, we should recall that we glory in it because joy in time and eternity was won for us by that love of which the Cross is now the symbol.

14. The Joy of Pain

People do not go out in search of discomfort or pain. On the contrary, a good part of the energy expended by human beings is used in an effort to avoid suffering. Many people make their living through pursuits that have as their purpose the lessening of discomfort in their fellowman.

Christ presents no greater challenge to pleasure-loving human nature than in holding out hardship as a blessing. Of one form of suffering, persecution, he says: "Blessed are you, when men revile you, and persecute you, and speak all manner of evil against you falsely, because of me. Be glad and light-hearted, for a rich reward awaits you in heaven. . . ." (Matt. 5:11-12) This promise can be applied to his whole teaching regarding the blessing of pain.

We can make little spiritual progress unless we find joy in our tribulations. Resignation is only the first step. We have not arrived at a true understanding of the teaching of Christ if we do not see reasons for rejoicing in our trials. The paradox of joy in pain is succinctly expressed in a phrase of St. Paul: ". . . sad men, that rejoice continually" (II Cor. 6:10).

Nobody in the history of the Church understood this seeming contradiction better than St. Paul, and nobody has expressed it with greater clarity. He makes it clear to the Corinthians that we are far from rejoicing in pain for its own sake. Only the abnormal would do this. It is the effect of our suffering that gives us reason for joy. This idea is illustrated by St. Paul's reference to the effects of a correction that he had had to administer to the Corinthians: ". . . even if I caused you pain by my letter, I am not sorry for it. Perhaps I was tempted to feel sorry, when I saw how my letter had caused you even momentary pain, but now I am glad: not glad of the pain, but glad of the repentance the pain brought with it." (II Cor. 7:8-9)

The reward of suffering is never far from St. Paul's mind. He is willing to accept endless difficulties and pains because he knows that tribulations are the price of eternal joy and glory. "Though the outward part of our nature is being worn down," he writes to the Corinthians, "our inner life is refreshed from day to day. This light and momentary affliction brings with it a reward multiplied every way, loading us with everlasting glory; if only we will fix our eyes on what is unseen, not on what we can see. What we can see, lasts but for a moment; what is unseen is eternal." (II Cor. 4:16-18)

The same doctrine is found in the writings and sayings of that wise virgin, St. Therese, who turned so much pain into such indescribable glory. She reached a point where she could say: "I wish for neither suffering nor death, although both are precious to me, and I have long called on them as messengers of joy." She wrote that her life in the convent was strewn with thorns rather than roses. She suffered such trials as the temptation to doubt the existence of heaven, on which she had set her heart so intently, the temptation to feel that she had no vocation to the convent, and this the very day before her profession as a nun. During her last illness, even a whisper caused her pain, and the physician attending her told the other nuns he had never seen anybody suffer so intensely with such patience. Every pain became for her a messenger of joy, because each was a manifestation of the will of the God she loved with all her heart. She knew that anything he willed must not only be good for her, but the very best that he could send her.

Centuries ago, David expressed beautifully the value God sets on our suffering: "No tear of mine but thou dost hoard and record it" (Ps. 55:9). To those who are surprised that God should ask us to go through tribulation, Julian of Norwich says: "He said not: thou shalt not be troubled—thou shalt not be tempted—thou shalt not be distressed; but he said: thou shalt not be overcome."

The plain truth is that the crown can be gained only through the Cross. There is no other way to glory for us than that traversed by our Lord. St. Paul explains the sequence: "Yours is to be the same mind which Christ Jesus showed. His nature is, from the first, divine, and yet he did not see, in the rank of Godhead, a prize to be coveted; he dispossessed himself, and took the nature of a slave, fashioned in the likeness of men, and presenting himself to us in human form; and then he lowered his own dignity, accepted an obedience which brought him to death, death on a cross. That is why God has raised him to such a height, given him that name which is greater than any other name; so that everything in heaven and on earth and under the earth must bend the knee before the name of Jesus, and every tongue must confess Jesus Christ as the Lord, dwelling in the glory of God the Father." (Phil. 2:5-11)

The very idea of resurrection implies death. The joy

of the one depends on the other. Christ links his suffering and his rising from the dead when he says: "This my Father loves in me, that I am laying down my life, to take it up again afterwards" (Jn. 10:17).

Failure saddens and depresses most people. The Cross appeared to indicate failure, but it turned out to be the instrument of the greatest triumph in the history of the world. So convinced of this were the early followers of our Lord that we find Paul and Barnabas rejoicing when their apparent success in converting the men of the Pisidian Antioch turned into a rout. When the chief citizens stirred up a persecution against them, "they shook off the dust from their feet as they left them, and went on to Iconium." Immediately the author of the Acts comments: "The disciples, meanwhile, were filled with rejoicing, and with the Holy Spirit." (Acts 13:51-52)

We cannot desire anything better from God than that which he willed for his own Son. Our Lord saw beyond the Cross the joyous results for himself and for the race which he had come to ransom. The author of the Epistle to the Hebrews urges us to consider the way in which Christ endured his Passion because of the gladness that would flow from it. "Let us fix our eyes on Jesus," he says, "the origin and the crown of all faith, who, to win his prize of blessedness, endured the cross and made light of its shame, Jesus, who now sits on the right of God's throne" (Heb. 12:2).

Those who possess the mind of Christ rejoice in their tribulations, not only because the effect will be an increase of their own glory, but also because through their acceptance of suffering they can help others to reach eternal happiness. So completely are we one with Christ in his Mystical Body, the Church, that he unites our crosses with his Cross, our sacrifices with his sacrifice, our acts of atonement with his act of Redemption. Thus St. Paul could write: "I am glad of my sufferings on your behalf, as, in this mortal frame of mine, I help to pay off the debt which the afflictions of Christ still leave to be paid, for the sake of his body, the Church" (Col. 1:24).

Since our Lord paid in full the debt of our transgressions, the way in which we are able to atone for sin is shrouded in mystery. That we are able to offer atonement is obvious from Holy Scripture, as well as from the traditional teaching of the Church. Our Lady is called coredemptrix because of her pre-eminent participation in the Redemption wrought by Christ. We also have a role in our Lord's redemptive sacrifice. We can all make our own these other words of St. Paul: "But even if I am made the libation for the sacrifice and service of your faith, I joy and rejoice with you. And in the same way do you also joy and rejoice with me." (Phil. 2:17, CV)

Those who truly love, desire above all the good of those loved. We have it in our power to bring to others the priceless good of God's grace through the sacrifices which we offer for them. We may feel that we have enough sins of our own for which to atone, and that it would be arrogant even to think of atoning for the sins of others. Although St. Paul realized that he had sins of his own that required atonement, he could still write about making up in his body for the Church those things which were lacking in the Passion of Christ.

Men will endure great hardship if they have a strong enough motive. Jacob was bargaining for strenuous labor when he agreed to work for Laban for seven years in order to win Laban's daughter, Rachel. Scripture says: "So Jacob served seven years for Rachel, and they seemed to him but a few days because of his love for her" (Gen. 29:20, CV).

A child may not be able to understand the benefits of an operation, but he will submit to it readily if he is assured of its good effects by his parents. We are all children before God, and we need only to be convinced that he will extract from our sufferings the most joyful effects in order to welcome our trials, not only with resignation, but with a measure of serene joy.

Each of us can take as addressed to himself the words of Proverbs: "My son, do not undervalue the correction the Lord sends thee, do not be unmanned when he reproves thy faults. It is where he loves that he bestows correction, like a father whose son is dear to him." (Prov. 3:11)

The theme of Dante's *Divine Comedy* is found in the beautiful phrase: *In His Will is our peace.* In his peace is our joy. The fact that we cannot understand his purpose in a particular trial need not lessen our gladness in carrying out his will. We expect too much if we ask him to reveal his exact purpose, as well as his will. It should be sufficient that we understand that his general purpose in our tribulations is our purification. If his purpose is not always clear, his will is ever manifest. Our merit would be lessened if his whole plan were laid out before us, because then there would be less room for the faith and trust which he has shown to be so important. St. Therese would not have been in a position to give the Church her doctrine of abandonment if God had explained to her step by step the purpose of the trials to which he asked her to submit.

As, in the natural order, flowers yield their full perfume only when crushed, so in the spiritual order we find fulfillment only when our wills have been crushed and refashioned to match the Master Will, from which flows all peace and joy, both in this world and in the world awaiting us.

There was a spiritual abyss between a hedonist writer like Oscar Wilde and a foundress of a religious order like Catherine McAuley. And yet there is a remarkable similarity in the way they express their recognition of the value of pain. "There are times," wrote Wilde, "when Sorrow seems to be the only truth. Other things may be illusions of the eye or appetite, made to blind the one and cloy the other, but out of Sorrow have the worlds been built." Mother McAuley, writing to one of the superiors of the Sisters of Mercy, expressed herself thus: "But without the Cross the real crown cannot come. Some great thing, which he designs to accomplish, would have been too much without a little bitterness in the cup. Bless and love the Fatherly Hand, which has hurt you. He will soon come with both hands filled with blessings."

15. *The Joy of Prayer*

The deepest joy in the natural order comes from being in the company of those we love. The mass movement that takes place on national holidays is evidence of this truth. To reach home, to enjoy the presence of loved ones, people will travel hundreds, and thousands, of miles. If it is impossible to be together physically, every effort is made to commune by telephone.

The purest joy in the spiritual order is to be in the company of him who has made himself our Father, Brother and Friend. We enter into his company through prayer. We are ever in his presence, but we become conscious that he is present only when we raise our minds and hearts to him in prayer. "One cry to the Lord . . . one word of summons to my God, and he, from his sanctuary, listened to my voice," testified David, who left us in his psalms a treasury of prayer. Again he says: "Thou wilt make me full of joy in thy presence." (Ps. 17:7, 15:11)

The gladness that prayer is capable of bringing us can be understood only if we remember that God has established between himself and us the relationship of Friend to friend. No relationship, not even that between husband and wife, or between parents and children, can be satisfying unless it includes the esteem, respect and affection that characterize friendship. If a marriage is to be happy, husband and wife must be friends before they become spouses, and the qualities of friendship must endure throughout their married life. Only then will there be added to physical union the note of mental and spiritual communion.

The essence of our joy in prayer is that we can talk with our God, as friend with Friend. We cannot fail to be impressed by the way in which our Lord uses the term *friend,* or *friendship,* in speaking of our relationship with each of the three Persons of the Trinity. Of the friendship of the Father, he says: ". . . you will make your requests in my name; and there is no need for me to tell you that I will ask the Father to grant them to you, because the

Father himself is *your friend,* since you have become *my friends* . . ." (Jn. 16:26, 27). Of his friendship for the disciples, and for us, he says: ". . . I have made known to you all that my Father has told me; and so I have called you *my friends*" (Jn. 15:15). And of the Holy Spirit, he says: "He who is to *befriend you,* the Holy Spirit . . . will in his turn make everything plain . . ." (Jn. 14:26).

In human affairs, it is considered a great advantage to have *a friend at court.* We not only have such friends at the court of heaven as our Lady and the saints, but repeated assurances from the Divine and Eternal King that he is waiting with friendly eagerness to have us come before his throne, ready to accept our prayer, whether it take the form of adoration, contrition, thanksgiving or petition.

As we offer His Divine Majesty our prayer of adoration, thus recognizing him as the Giver and Sustainer of our very life, the awe that we naturally feel in his presence is blended with the joy we experience in the realization that he wants graciously to receive our adoration. With both astonishment and exultation, we make our own the prayer of David: "Lord, what is Adam's race, that thou givest heed to it; what is man, that thou carest for him?" (Ps. 143:3).

We cannot forget, of course, that the King of the heavenly court is not only the God to whom we owe adoration, but the Father and Friend whom we so often offend. For this reason, we must join to the prayer of adoration that of contrition. However, even the prayer of contrition, synonymous as contrition is with sorrow, is not without its element of gladness. The quiet joy of the prayer of contrition is best understood by consideration of the sadness experienced by a fundamentally religious person when his conscience reproaches him for some infidelity toward the God who has so constantly extended to him love and friendship. One who has betrayed God's friendship through sin has only to think of his Savior's words to his disciples in Gethsemani to be overcome with remorse: "My soul, he said, is ready to die with sorrow" (Matt. 26:38). The erring friend of Christ can suppose his Master reproaching him in the words of Ecclesiasticus: "Death itself cannot match it for sadness, when friend and companion becomes thy enemy" (Ecclus. 35:1).

When we think of it, we must always be astounded that God is unwearied in waiting for us to come to him with the prayer of contrition on our lips. Seventy times seven, we can offer the psalmist's prayer of repentance, and he will receive it: "Here, O God, is my sacrifice, a broken spirit; a heart that is humbled and contrite, thou, O God, wilt never disdain" (Ps. 50:19).

God wants, however, to give us far more than forgiveness. He is not merely our merciful Judge, but our omnipotent and loving Father. He wants us to be ambitious for his graces and favors. He wants us to ask him for the spiritual riches which he alone can bestow. His eagerness to give us everything that is good for us is the reason for our joy in the prayer of petition.

It was in order to leave no doubt about God's ardent desire to receive and grant our prayer of petition that our Lord said to his disciples: "Believe me, you have only to make any request of the Father in my name, and he will grant it to you. Until now, you have not been making any requests in my name; make them, and they will be granted, to bring you gladness in full measure." (Jn. 16:23, 24) Christ made this statement just before he emphasized the relationship of Friend to friend that the Father had deigned to assume.

The power of the prayer of petition was one of our

Lord's favorite themes. He said to the Jews: "Among yourselves, if a father is asked by his son for bread, will he give him a stone? Or for a fish, will he give him a snake instead of a fish? Or if he is asked for an egg, will he give him a scorpion? Why then, if you, evil as you are, know well enough how to give your children what is good for them, is not your Father much more ready to give, from heaven, his gracious Spirit to those who ask him?" (Lk. 11:11-13) We should observe that the gift of God's Spirit is the supreme gift. If he will give us the supreme gift, it goes without saying that he will give us all lesser gifts that may be good for us.

God wants us to go to him as a child will go to his parents. What does a child tell his father and mother, except that he has fallen and bruised himself? What does he confide to his parents but that he is hungry, or thirsty, or sick, or that somebody has given him a difficult time? These are the things we can tell our heavenly Father in prayer. He is the only one who can heal the spiritual bruises that we have suffered from our falls into sin. If we have bruised our minds through sins against the truth, if we have bruised our hearts through sins of waywardness, he is waiting to make everything right again. If we hunger for truth, if we thirst for love, he has the truth that will satisfy our hunger, he has the love that will slake our thirst. If people, or circumstances, have made things difficult for us, he will give us the strength to surmount the difficulties.

God's satisfaction in man's prayer, and his instant answer to it, are illustrated in a joyous encounter that the Prophet Daniel had with the Angel Gabriel. Daniel thus addressed God: "To those who love thee, so gracious. . . . No merits of ours, nothing but thy great love emboldens us to lay our prayers at thy feet. Thy hearing, Lord, and thy pardon; thy heed, Lord, and thy aid." God's answer was instantaneous. With an immediacy which caused Daniel to tremble with awe, the Angel Gabriel was at his side, revealing truths concerning the coming of Christ. "Even as thy prayer began," Gabriel told him, "a secret was disclosed, and I am here to make it known to thee, so well heaven loves thee." (Dan. 9:4, 18, 19, 23)

The power of continued prayer is shown in Daniel's having a second colloquy with Gabriel. The prophet says: "I looked up, and saw a man standing there clad all in linen, and his girdle of fine gold. Clear as topaz his body was, like the play of lightning shone his face, and like burning cressets his eyes; arms and legs of him had the sheen of bronze, and when he spoke, it was like the murmur of a throng. The vision was for me, for Daniel, alone. . . . Daniel, said he; thy prayers did not go unheard. Prayer of thine it was beckoned me to thy side, from the moment when thou didst set about thy search for knowledge, by fasting in the presence of thy God. . . ." (Dan. 10:5-7, 12)

The Christ whose coming Gabriel discussed with Daniel came almost two thousand years ago. We have had the joy of receiving him and his word. But often we do not receive the full measure of joy of which he spoke because we do not accept literally his clear promise: ". . . ask, and the gift will come, seek, and you shall find; knock, and the door shall be opened to you. Everyone that asks, will receive, that seeks, will find, that knocks, will have the door opened to him." (Lk. 11:9, 10)

There are only three conditions for experiencing the joy of answered prayer: that we obey God's law, that we ask with confidence, and that what we ask be good for us.

We cannot expect God to listen to our prayers if our hearts are far from him through disobedience to his law.

The writer of the Book of Proverbs explains why God must remain deaf to the pleas of those who break his commandments: "From the wicked man's sacrifice the Lord turns away with loathing; only the just with their vows win his favor" (Prov. 15:8). The psalmist asks: "Would God listen to me, if my heart were set on wrong?" (Ps. 65:18). Of the prayer of the just man, St. James says: "When a just man prays fervently, there is great virtue in his prayer" (Jas. 5:16). And St. John observes: "Beloved, if conscience does not condemn us, we can appear boldly before God, and he will grant all our requests" (I Jn. 3:21, 22).

The power of prayer that is offered with complete confidence is manifest in the striking declaration of our Lord: "I tell you, then, when you ask anything in prayer, *you have only to believe that it is yours, and it will be granted you*" (Mk. 11:24). We do not honor God if we ask his benefits while entertaining doubts regarding either his power to do what we ask, or his loving eagerness to bestow upon us everything that is good for us. "Such familiar confidence we have in him," says St. John, "that we believe he listens to us whenever we make any request of him in accordance with his will. We are sure he listens to all our requests, sure that the requests we make of him will be granted." (I Jn. 5:14, 15)

St. James emphasizes the efficacy of trustful prayer and the futility of prayer offered without confidence. He is writing about prayer for the gift of wisdom, but what he says applies to any prayer of petition: "Is there one of you who still lacks wisdom? God gives to all, freely and ungrudgingly; so let him ask God for it, and the gift will come. (Only it must be in faith that he asks, he must not hesitate; one who hesitates is like a wave out at sea, driven to and fro by the wind; such a man must not hope to win any gift from God.)" (Jas. 1:5-7)

Perhaps St. James was thinking of the way in which St. Peter started to walk over the Sea of Galilee, only to sink because he concentrated on the violence of the wind and waves, rather than on the power of God to sustain him. When Peter discovered that the figure approaching the disciples' wind-tossed ship during the night was not an apparition, but Christ walking over the water, the impetuous Apostle called out: "Lord, if it is thyself, bid me come to thee over the water." Our Lord replied with one word, "Come." Thus Peter's prayer was instantly granted, and he had the thrill of walking over the sea as though it were solid ground. "Then, seeing how strong the wind was, he lost courage and began to sink; whereupon he cried aloud, Lord, save me. And Jesus at once stretched out his hand and caught hold of him, saying to him, Why didst thou hesitate, man of little faith?" (Matt. 14:25-31)

Once Peter had cut off, through doubt, the supernatural power that had supported him as he walked over the sea, he had to depend on the natural support of our Lord's outstretched hand. If we realized how we forfeit the joy of answered prayer by allowing the winds and waves of doubt to blow through our minds and hearts while we offer our petitions to God, we would pray for the kind of faith and trust manifested by those who were cured by Jesus during his public ministry.

When our Lord performed miracles of healing, he told those whom he cured that they had been restored to health because of the faith with which they had made their requests. A good example is the case of the blind man who heard that our Savior was passing by, and cried out: "Jesus, Son of David, have pity on me!" When the

Lord asked what the man would have him do, and the blind man answered, "Lord, give me back my sight," Jesus said, "thy faith has brought thee recovery." The Gospel says that "all at once he recovered his sight." (Mk. 10:47, 51, 52)

When a miracle takes place, people appear astounded at such a manifestation of the power and goodness of God. The fact is that miracles would occur more often if we had greater confidence in God's infinite power and his desire to give us everything that is good for us.

Regarding the third condition for being heard by God, namely, that we ask only for those things which are good for us, it should be obvious that our Father would not give us anything which he sees to be an obstacle to our spiritual good. To those who ask for strictly temporal favors, without any reference to spiritual goods, St. James says: ". . . what you ask for is denied you, because you ask for it with ill intent; you would squander it on your appetites" (Jas. 4:3).

Not only is there nothing wrong with asking for proper temporal favors, but we actually honor God by requesting them. Sometimes a person who is chronically sick will be asked whether he has prayed for a cure, and reply that he would never ask God for any but purely spiritual graces. Such a person appears to be implying that our Lord perhaps made a mistake when he answered the pleas of those who asked for physical cures, or that our Lady is mistaken whenever she obtains a miraculous cure for some sick client of hers at Lourdes or Guadalupe.

The Church gives us a lead concerning prayer for temporal things in the liturgy. A good example is found in the Mass for the Wednesday of the Fourth Week of Lent, in which the secret and postcommunion prayers ask for earthly, as well as heavenly, blessings. In the secret prayer, the Church prays: *We beseech thee, Almighty God, that having been cleansed of our sins by this sacrifice, we may receive from thee true health of mind and body. Through Jesus Christ, thy Son, our Lord. . . .* The postcommunion prayer offers this petition: *May the sacrament which we have received, O Lord, our God, nourish us spiritually, and support us with temporal aid. Through Jesus Christ. . . .* These prayers make it evident that the Church wants us to rejoice in physical blessings, as well as in spiritual ones, since both body and soul come from God.

A study of the petitions of the Lord's Prayer shows us that, in our prayers, we must place first things first. We begin by asking that our heavenly Father be glorified by having his name hallowed, that his rule be established in souls by their reception of his kingship, that his will be done perfectly on earth, as it is in heaven. Then we go on to ask that he bestow on us the necessities of daily life, that we be loosed from the chains of sin by having our trespasses against his law forgiven, while we promise to forgive those who have trespassed against us, and that we be given the strength to surmount temptation.

There is one petition that sums up all others. It may be expressed in the prayer: *Lord, give us the grace to do your will perfectly.* It is his will that we believe and hope in him. It is his will that we love him, and that we love our fellowman, and that we show this love by keeping the Commandments, the first of which concern our obligations toward him, and the others our duties toward our neighbor. It is his will that we overcome temptation because we cannot keep his law unless we conquer the allurements of the world, the flesh and the devil. It is his will that we grow in union with him through a spirit of prayer. This is why we say that if we ask only for the grace to do and accept his will as perfectly as possible in our present state, we are asking for everything that is conducive to fulfilling his purpose in our regard. Fulfilling his will perfectly, of course, means perfect joy.

A great deal of joy is taken out of our prayer if we pray with tension. People express concern that they have not prayed at certain times that they suppose prayer is prescribed. Morning and evening prayer is strongly recommended, but there is no commandment: *Thou shalt say thy morning and evening prayers.* We have a general obligation to pray, because we need God's grace very much, but the times of prayer are not specified, except for religious, whose Rule dictates that they pray together at certain hours of the day or night. The Church recommends, but does not command, priests to read their breviary at hours that are considered appropriate for the different parts of the divine office. Members of the laity will sometimes state apologetically that they omitted their *morning prayers,* but spoke with God during their work later. They can be sure that God is highly pleased with such an arrangement.

Since temptation presents the great threat to our carrying out God's will, we do have an obligation to pray in time of temptation. Our Lord indicated the great importance of prayer in temptation when he said to the Apostles in Gethsemani: "Watch and pray, that you may not enter into temptation; the spirit is willing enough, but the flesh is weak" (Mk. 14:38). We would be fools not to recognize the threat to our temporal and eternal joy that lies in temptation. Writing about the special providence that God exercises toward some young men and women who reach high sanctity, calling them from earthly life in their youth, the writer of the Book of Wisdom says: "Divine favor, divine love . . . caught him away, before wickedness could pervert his thoughts, before wrong-doing could allure his heart; such witchery evil has, to tarnish honor, such alchemy do the roving passions exercise even on minds that are true metal . . ." (Wis. 4:12). The Church gives us a realistic prayer against temptation in the Mass of Ember Wednesday in September: *Succor, in thy Mercy, our weakness, O Lord: and, in pity, renew that poor strength of ours which, of its nature, is ever wasting away. Through Jesus Christ, thy Son, our Lord.*

The Church reminds us not to neglect the prayer of thanksgiving by placing on the lips of priests and people, during Mass and the divine office, the exclamation: *Thanks be to God.* This prayer occurs three times during Mass, and after every hour of the office. Saying *thank you* brings joy to both the person who says it and to the person who hears it. Unfortunately, however, many take the favors of God and man for granted. Often, those who are blessed with the good things of life, good health, good friends, a good living, which are all God's gifts, never think of saying: *Thank you, Lord.* It seems never to occur to them that the offering of thanks is not only a matter of courtesy but a matter of obligation. The fact is that we *owe* God thanks. When only one of ten lepers cured by our Lord came back to express his gratitude for so great a blessing, Jesus reproachfully said: "Were not all ten made clean? And the other nine, where are they? Not one has come back to give God the praise, except this stranger." (Lk. 17:13-19)

If we are to experience the full joy of prayer, we must develop some degree of familiarity in our conversation with God. Since God has made it clear that he is ready to deal with us in terms of friendship, we deprive ourselves of much gladness by speaking to him with the formality which friends spontaneously dispense with. If we always have to read to God from prayer books, or have to be ever addressing him through prayers that we know by memory, we will not feel the joy that prompted the writer of the Book of Proverbs to say: "Sweeter than ointment, sweeter than any perfume, when man's heart talks to heart of friend" (Prov. 27:9).

Of course we will never stop using prayer books. The missal and the breviary are books of prayer. Neither will we ever forego saying the wonderful prayer that our Lord gave us, the *Our Father,* nor the beautiful and powerful prayer, the *Hail Mary.* But God wants us, at least occasionally, to talk things over with him in our own words, in heart-to-heart conversation. We can do this wherever we are, in church, at home, in our place of work, in an automobile, subway train, or wherever we happen to be.

Laymen and laywomen who would be startled by a suggestion that they engage in meditation or mental prayer often are making meditation and mental prayer without realizing it. Prayer, in general, is defined as raising the mind and heart to God. Any application of the mind to God, or the things of God, is meditation. There is unsuspected joy in thinking about God and his truth. This is evident from the satisfaction that men and women express at the end of a mission or retreat. They have been doing a great deal of spiritual thinking, and they are surprised and delighted with its effects. Perhaps their reaction is best conveyed in an expression that is often used: *it never struck me that way before.*

The importance of such spiritual thinking is evident from the fact that the quality of our thoughts determines the quality of our minds. As an ancient philosopher put it: "Such as is the habit of thy thought, so will be the color of thy mind, for the mind is dyed by the thought."

Furthermore, the quality of our minds determines the quality of our actions. Truthful thoughts lead us to act truthfully with others. Peaceful thoughts make us men of peace. Merciful thoughts prompt us to deal mercifully with our fellowmen. Charitable thoughts inspire us to act charitably toward those around us. Thoughts of eternity prepare us for eternal life.

The thinking we do in meditation should lead to that speaking with God which characterizes mental prayer. Thinking about God, and the things of God, is merely preparation for talking with God. Such talking with God is the supreme joy during our earthly sojourn.

A natural question arises concerning our joy in prayer when we think of the dryness that we all feel so frequently when striving to commune with our heavenly Father and Friend. Aridity seems to take all joy out of prayer. We are reassured by a statement of St. Therese, who surely mastered the art of prayer. Writing of the dryness she frequently felt during her thanksgiving after Communion, she said: "I should not rejoice in my dryness of soul but rather attribute it to my lack of fervor and fidelity. I suppose I ought to be worried because I so often fall asleep during meditation and thanksgiving after Holy Communion, but I reflect that little children are just as dear to their parents, asleep or awake; that the Lord *knows our frame: he remembers that we are dust.*"

When we are discouraged because we think we are making no progress in prayer, we should understand that we are progressing by the very effort we make to pray. If we only strive to pray, the Holy Spirit will supply for our weakness, as St. Paul says: "The Spirit comes to the aid of our weakness; when we do not know what prayer to offer, to pray as we ought, the Spirit himself intercedes for us . . ." (Rom. 8:26).

To assure ourselves of permanent joy in prayer, we have to strive to grow in a habit of prayer, or a spirit of prayer. A spirit of prayer makes it second nature to turn to God and converse with him. It causes us to breathe as naturally in the supernatural atmosphere of the spiritual world as we breathe in the atmosphere around us. If we live in an atmosphere of prayer now, it will be easy for us to make the transition from the joy of communing with God in this life to the joy of union with him for all eternity.

16. The Joy of the Liturgy

We experience joy in giving expression to our thoughts and feelings, particularly if we are deeply moved by what we think and feel. We enjoy talking because it is the main means we have for expressing ourselves. The overwhelming desire that human beings have to manifest their thoughts and emotions accounts for expressions like *I am so happy, I want to sing,* or *I feel so happy, I could dance.* Writing about the urgency that we experience in giving expression to the emotion of love, St. Augustine said that to sing is the work of a lover.

The liturgy is a source of joy to those who strive for union with God because it gives expression to our thoughts and feelings about God. In using the phrase, *our thoughts and feelings about God,* we are not referring to personal and individual thoughts about him, such as characterize private prayer, but the thought and feeling of the whole Church.

Pope Paul VI, when cardinal-archbishop of Milan, wrote to his priests in a pastoral letter on the liturgy: "We desire that you understand and meditate the aptitude of the sacred liturgy for becoming, once more, *the expression of the people's soul.*" By saying that "in our relations with God we must become capable again of dialogue," he was making it clear that the liturgy involves not only the Church addressing herself to God, but God also addressing himself to the Church. There is not much joy in conversation that is mainly onesided. One of the reasons for our joy in the liturgy is that it is the divinely appointed means through which God talks to us, as well as the means through which we talk to God. The liturgy, if we understand it properly, constitutes a joyful dialogue between God and man.

In this dialogue, we have an interlocutor who partakes of the nature of God and the nature of man, Christ, God's Son and our Brother. He is spokesman for God and for man. He declares God's truth to us through the liturgy, and he presents whatever is true in our minds and hearts to God, also through the liturgy.

Christ became man in order to change man. Christ alone changes people directly; others change people only indirectly, through psychological influence. He changed us first through baptism. He continues to change us by means of the actual graces that accompany the liturgical reading and hearing of his Word. His Word prepares us for the greater change that is wrought in us by means of the liturgical rites. We rejoice to hear God's Word in the liturgy. But our joy would be incomplete if the liturgical action did not bring us into God's presence and give us a participation in his life.

Pope Paul, in his Milan pastoral, said that the liturgy "is the most powerful (prayer), because it contains not only the human cry of entreaty but the operative Presence of God." *The human cry of entreaty* is not just that of us poor wayfarers, who enter God's presence with a consciousness of our misery and unworthiness. We look up during the liturgy, and we realize that "here is Jesus, the spokesman of the new covenant, and the sprinkling of his blood, which has better things to say than Abel's had" (Heb. 12:24). In the liturgy, we have *the operative Presence of God* because "Jesus continues forever, and his priestly office is unchanging. . . . This high priest of ours is one who has taken his seat in heaven, on the right hand of that throne where God sits in majesty, ministering, now, in the sanctuary, in that true tabernacle which the Lord, not man, has set up." (Heb. 7:24, 8:1-2)

Because Christ "lives on still to make intercession on our behalf," we have the joy of conversing with God (Heb. 7:25). This spokesman of ours is the well-beloved Son. It is hardly surprising that God immediately replies, speaking graciously to us who now form one body with his Son.

God speaks to us in two ways through the liturgy. He first speaks through the Word which we call Sacred Scripture, and then through the Word whom we call Christ. This is a double aspect of one mystery, the mystery of Christ. It is said of those who were converted to Christ on the first Pentecost that they "occupied themselves continually with the apostles' teaching, their fellowship in the breaking of bread, and the fixed times of prayer" (Acts 2:42). The preaching of the Apostles, like all preaching through the centuries, was the breaking of the bread of God's revealed Word. The other breaking of the bread, for which the first was a preparation, was the celebration of the Eucharist, in which the Church receives the living Bread that has come down from heaven.

In the liturgy, Christ is present under the species of Sacred Scripture and under the species of bread and wine. It was this which prompted Pope John XXIII to say at the beginning of his pontificate that the *Bible* and the *Chalice* are at the heart of Christian life.

Pope Pius XII, in the encyclical *Mediator Dei,* called by Pope Paul *the magna charta of the Church's liturgical renewal,* stated that the liturgy is "the worship rendered by the Mystical Body in the entirety of its Head and members." The members of Christ's Body, the Church, can find the joy of fulfillment only if joined to their Head, just as in our physical bodies the hand or foot depends for the fulfillment of its purpose on the head. Pope Pius could not have been more emphatic in showing how this doctrine applies to our union with Christ in the liturgy. He wrote that "all the faithful make up a single and compact body with Christ for its Head, and that the Christian community is bound to *participate* in the liturgical rites according to their station."

It was Pope Paul, as cardinal-archbishop of Milan, who italicized the word *participate* in the foregoing quotation. A note of excitement runs through the Milan pastoral as the author shows that the idea of participation occurs on every page of *Mediator Dei.* As a matter of fact, he states that the aim of the encyclical is "precisely *the participation of the faithful in the liturgical rites.*"

The same sense of urgency regarding participation of the laity in the liturgical rites characterizes the Constitution on the Liturgy adopted by the bishops at the Second Vatican Council, and promulgated by Pope Paul with such deep and evident satisfaction at the end of the Council's second session.

"Mother Church earnestly desires," declares the constitution, "that all the faithful should be led to that full, conscious, and active participation in liturgical celebrations which is demanded by the very nature of the liturgy. . . .

"In the restoration and promotion of the sacred liturgy," the constitution continues, *"this full and active participation by all the people is the aim to be considered above all else . . ."* (italics added). "Pastors of souls must, therefore, realize that, when the liturgy is celebrated, something more is required than the mere observance of the laws governing valid and licit celebration; it is their duty also to insure that the faithful take part fully aware of what they are doing, actively engaged in the rite, and enriched by its effects."

The joy of participation in the Mass, which is the core of the liturgy, is shown by the satisfaction that has come to the laity through the habitual use of the English missal. The way in which so many carry, arrange and use their missals is indicative of the value they place on this means of participation in the liturgy. Their attitude toward the missal indicates that they have discovered spiritual riches of which they had hardly been conscious. They saw that the apt and varied texts from Scripture, and the prayers, so meaningful and graceful, constituted a feast, intellectual, emotional and spiritual.

Instead of looking at the altar with a combined feeling of puzzlement and patience, the laity began to understand that the visible priest was acting in the place of the invisible and eternal High Priest. It was becoming clear to them that Christ's earthly minister was continuing, as the Milan pastoral expressed it, "the mediating mission of Christ, God and Man, Priest and Victim redemptive of the human race, unique and eternal Priest of redeemed mankind, ever living and working in the priesthood transfused into His Mystical Body, the Church."

The interest of the laity in the revised liturgy of Holy Week is another indication of their eagerness for an ever increasing participation in the public worship of the Church. They have discovered the joy of being participators rather than observers. It was partly this aroused interest in the liturgy which moved the bishops of the Second Vatican Council to approve the use of the vernacular in many parts of the Mass, and in the administration of the sacraments.

It is likely that many of those who are rejoicing in an increased participation in the liturgy have not adverted very much to the fact that one of the reasons for their joy is that they are learning more about their religion through such participation. After stating that "participation involves *seeing and hearing,*" the Milan pastoral letter pointed out that "with her holy signs, the Church has placed at the disposal of liturgical piety a very rich material alphabet." It explained that "the liturgy demonstrates a stupendous formative capacity, an ability to take over the religious instruction of children and adults, of plain folk and men of culture, and make it effective."

Once the door had been opened to the often unrecognized riches of the liturgy, the laity became conscious of the inestimable treasury of the liturgical cycle. Having found such joy in the rich texts of the Sunday Masses, they were ready to explore what the liturgy had to offer in the celebration of various mysteries of the Faith, and of the feasts of our Lady and the saints.

Here, in a varied dramatic setting, the members of the Church could watch unfolding the whole history of God's dealing with his marvelous creature, man. Not only could they watch this Creator-creature interchange, but they were made to feel that they were part of it. In the liturgy, they found a reflection of the joys and sorrows of human life. The liturgy never permitted them, however, to forget that for those who truly became one with Christ, all the sorrow would in the end be dissipated by the joy of resurrection and eternal life.

Even while the Church has her ministers don the purple of repentance as the ecclesiastical year opens with the season of Advent, her long-range purpose is to show that the inexpressible yearning of fallen man for reunion with his God finds fulfillment in the coming of Christ, Pontifex, bridge-builder between God and man, between the visible and the invisible worlds, between time and eternity. Because the fruit of the Spirit who animates her is joy, the Church will not allow the somber season of Advent to reach the halfway mark without interjecting a note of joy. She opens the Mass of Gaudete Sunday with the happy greeting once addressed to the Philippians: "Joy to you in the Lord at all times; once again I wish you joy" (4:4).

After allowing her members to feel something of the pain of separation from God during the four weeks of Advent, the Church helps them to experience something of the joy of the shepherds when the glory of the Lord shone about them, and they listened ecstatically to angelic choirs, and to the news of great rejoicing, the birth of a Savior, the Lord Christ himself.

The member of the Church who will go to the trouble of reading the text of the three Masses of the feast of the birth of Christ will have the full wonder of the Incarnation break upon his mind. The Church takes him back in spirit to the eternal existence of the Word in the Father. She makes him realize, by recounting the physical events of the first Christmas night, what it meant for the Divine Word to step down from his celestial throne and live in time. The awe of the shepherds becomes the awe of the contemporary Church. That the joy of Christ's coming may find roots in the soul, the liturgy dwells on this central mystery during the octave of Christmas and through what is called twelfth night.

Swiftly, reminding us of the swiftness with which earthly life passes, we are carried by the liturgy to the threshold of Lent. Now we are reminded of our mortality as the Church places ashes on our foreheads. We are given to understand, through penitential exercises, what a bitter thing it is to turn from the Lord, our God. Lest we ever look lightly on sin again, the Church, like a strong and loving mother, puts our faces in the dust. The main purpose of the liturgy at this time is to impress us with the truth that sin deprives us of authentic joy on earth, and if persisted in, the joy of eternal union with God in heaven.

After five weeks of meditation on the galling slavery of sin, the liturgy brings us into that climactic week which is like a retreat for the whole Church. It is called Holy Week because it gives us participation in the holiest mysteries of our Faith.

The Church will not allow us to forget during this most sacred week the price that was paid for our temporal and eternal joy, the precious blood of the God-Man. The

Passion is read on four days, according to the four Gospels, with the final reading on Good Friday itself. So intent is the liturgy on highlighting the Passion at this time, that even on Holy Thursday, the Mass is concerned with the Cross rather than the Holy Eucharist, which the Church will honor with high joy later on the feast of Corpus Christi.

We are given the theme of the Holy Thursday liturgy in the introit of the Mass, which exclaims: *It behooves us to glory in the Cross of our Lord, Jesus Christ: in whom is our salvation, life and resurrection; by whom we are saved and delivered.* The preface of the Mass in also that of the Cross. And while the epistle contains St. Paul's account of the institution of the Holy Eucharist, the gospel narrates the washing of the Apostles' feet by our Lord. All this is preparation for the liturgy of the *Friday of the Lord's Passion.*

Although the Good Friday liturgy is celebrated in the black vestments of mourning, a note of joy is sounded as the ritual progresses. One of the antiphons announces that *through the Cross, joy has come to the whole world.* The priest sings on three successively higher tones, which thus become notes of victory, the antiphon: *Behold the wood of the Cross, on which hung the Savior of the world!*

What is particularly noticeable, even in the Good Friday liturgy, is that any overtone of excessive sadness or melancholy is excluded. We do not leave the ceremonies of this day of tragedy and triumph with a feeling of depression, but with one of joyous hope. The joy is muted because we have witnessed the indescribable torments of the innocent Son of God, but it is still there.

Then come the pensive hours of Holy Saturday, when we continue to mourn over the death of the first-born. We hover around the sepulchre in spirit. Our churches are strangely silent, as though we were awaiting an event about whose approach we had received news. The longing of our hearts is reflected in the new collect of the day: *Grant, we beseech thee, Lord, that we who look forward with devout longing to the resurrection of thy Son may obtain the glory of that resurrection. Through the same Christ, our Lord.*

The celebration of Easter begins in the evening of Holy Saturday, any time after sundown. On this holiest night of the year, the Church remains awake, to celebrate what St. Augustine calls *the mother of all the holy vigils.* During the first centuries, the members of the Church gathered to spend this entire night, from sunset to sunrise, in prayers, readings, and singing, commemorating the great victory of Light over darkness.

In the early Church, this watch was not just the commemoration of a past event, the resurrection of Christ, but also an anticipation of future glory. The first Christians associated this night, not only with our Lord's rising from the dead, but also with his second coming into the world.

There is no ceremony in the whole liturgy which causes a greater glow of joy than the Easter Vigil. The great paschal candle is carried in procession as a symbol of the risen Lord. An exultant note is struck when the Church prays: *May the light of Christ, gloriously risen, scatter the darkness of our minds!* There re-echoes through the church the joyful shout: *Lumen Christi!*

Then the Church tells the whole world, in the *Exsultet,* why she is rejoicing. The opening words of this majestic hymn proclaim the good news of the redemption of the human race: *It is truly right and fitting . . . to praise our*

Lord, Jesus Christ, who paid to the eternal Father in our place the debt that Adam had contracted, and, with his own blood, shed for us, blotted out the stain of the ancient guilt.

This night has been turned into day both because of the victory the Light won on this night, and because the victory of Christ, the Light, is the promise of our enjoyment of the Vision of God, in whose light we shall see light. Since we begin to share in Christ's victory over death through baptism, it is fitting that the liturgy once again makes this the baptismal night of the year. Through baptism, we are buried with him in order that we may rise with him. At one time, Lent was the period during which neophytes were put through the last stages of preparation for baptism. Now we are to regard Lent as a preparation for the annual commemoration of our baptism. This is why baptism is given such prominence in the Easter Vigil, and why we renew our baptismal vows during the liturgical service. The celebrant wears a white cope for the renewal ceremony because white is the symbol of joy. Baptism, we should note, is the sacrament which initiates us into all the joys that are ours through membership in the Mystical Body of Christ.

Finally, on this night of joy, we come to the climax of the liturgy, the Easter Mass, the preface of which concisely states the reasons for our joy: *By dying, he destroyed our death; by rising again, he restores our life.* The liturgy thus speaks of our Lord's Passion and his Resurrection in one breath, impressing upon us that they are two parts of the one action by which Christ atoned for the sins of mankind and restored it to the original pattern. The redemption wrought by Christ continues to produce its effects in us through the Mass, in which we eat and drink our redemption by eating the Paschal Lamb under the appearance of bread and wine.

It should be noted that Eastertide, with its *alleluias,* is longer than Lent, with its *misereres.* The better we understand the meaning and spirit of the liturgy, the clearer becomes the truth of St. Augustine's saying: "We are Easter men, and *alleluia* is our song."

The liturgical cycle brings us, fifty days after Easter, to another day of high joy, that of Pentecost, when the Church exults in the possession of God's Holy Spirit, the Spirit of the Father and the Son, the Spirit of truth, who guides her infallibly in the way of truth until the end of time. To impress upon us the importance of the action of the Divine Spirit in the Church, she forbids, during the octave of Pentecost, even the commemoration of the feast of a saint.

At the end of Pentecost's octave, we reach the feast which symbolizes the beginning and the end of all things, that of the Holy Trinity, in which we contemplate that God is all in all; we start with the Triune God, and finish with the Triune God, whom we hope to see in glorious vision during the endless ages of eternity.

After Trinity Sunday, there reaches out that long period which is called the season after Pentecost. During it, the Church, by the use of green in her vestments, emphasizes that this season of special peace symbolizes that immortal life which stretches before us like a vast tranquil sea, and to which we look forward with confident hope and serene joy.

17. The Joy of the Mass

Because the Holy Eucharist is, as Pius XII wrote, "the culmination and center of the Christian religion," our joy in the Eucharist is a climactic joy. Everything else in our religion leads up to the Eucharist. The other sacraments prepare us for participation in the eucharistic mystery. All private and public prayer, all other rites and services, should lead us to such participation.

Because on that day particularly we go back in spirit to the Last Supper, the gladness of Holy Thursday has a character all its own. We enter the supper-room and watch in awe as the table is cleared of everything but bread and wine. We share the exultation of the Apostles as we listen with them to the words which were to bring such indescribable joy to countless millions on their journey through this world: "Take, eat, this is my body. . . . Drink, all of you, of this; for this is my blood, of the new testament, shed for many, to the remission of sins. . . . Do this for a commemoration of me." (Matt. 26:27-28; Lk. 22:19)

Although the joy of Holy Thursday has a special quality, the essence of that joy is with us all during the year. Every church and chapel in which Christ re-enacts what he did at the Last Supper becomes a supper-room like its original at Jerusalem. The earth is encircled with such supper-rooms. Every altar on which Mass is offered is a supper table at which we sit with Christ as he gives himself to us in the eucharistic mystery.

Every day is for the Church both Holy Thursday and Good Friday. The Church rejoices that there is never a moment when Christ is not using the hands and the lips of some priest to provide for her members, not only the eucharistic banquet of the Last Supper, but also the eucharistic sacrifice of the Cross. The bread and wine are forever being changed into his body and blood by him of whom Scripture says: "We can claim a great high priest, and one who has passed right up through the heavens, Jesus Christ, the Son of God" (Heb. 4:14).

We experience satisfaction in the possession of priests on earth because the chief Priest makes himself present through his earthly ministers. The Mass is such a joyful ritual because in it Christ is exercising the primary function of priesthood, which is the offering of sacrifice. It is to emphasize that Christ is acting through his visible minister that the priest goes before the altar, not in his ordinary garb, but clothed from head to foot in the vestments of Christ's priesthood. St. Paul says that all who have been baptized in Christ's name "have put on the person of Christ" (Gal. 3:27). When he offers Mass, the human priest puts on the person of Christ in a new and more meaningful way.

Not only do we have the Son of God as priest, but also as sacrifice. In the Mass he continues the offering which he made on the Cross, and which he will continue to offer until the end of time. The connection between the Cross and the Mass is stressed by St. Paul when he writes: "So it is the Lord's death that you are heralding, whenever you eat this bread and drink this cup, until he comes" (I Cor. 11:26).

Instead of being saddened by the realization that his death is heralded in the eucharistic sacrifice, we rejoice in it. We are ever conscious that the high priest who is offering his body and blood on our altars rose from the dead, that he ascended into heaven and is seated at the right hand of the throne of God. We keep his sacrificial offering in the context of his resurrection and exaltation.

St. Paul speaks of heralding his death, as we speak of heralding good news, as we speak of the herald angels who announced the glad news of Christ's birth. The heralding of his death takes place in the Mass through the separate consecration of the bread and wine. When the bread is consecrated, it becomes the living body of Christ. When the wine is consecrated, it becomes the living blood of Christ. And since we cannot have his living blood without his living body, he is entirely present also under the appearance of wine. There could be no other purpose in the separate consecrations than the mystical re-presentation of his death.

In heralding our Lord's death, we are offering the perfect act of worship, encompassing adoration, atonement, petition and thanksgiving. It was not an accident that the Church started speaking of the *celebration* of Mass, and of the priest as the *celebrant*. Nothing in the world could afford greater reason for joyful celebration than the Mass. Nowhere can there be found more exultant music, more joyous use of light, greater artistic and architectural splendor, than that with which the Church surrounds the heralding of the sacrifice which her High Priest offers on her altars.

No sooner has the first sign of the cross been made in the Mass than the Church places on the lips of priest and people what amounts to a shout of joy: "I will go unto the altar of God, unto God who giveth joy to my youth" (Ps. 42:4, Douay).

One of the psalms beautifully expresses the adoration, atonement, petition and thanksgiving that are found in the Mass: "Let the whole earth keep holiday in God's honor; pay to the Lord the homage of your rejoicing, appear in his presence with glad hearts. . . . Pass through these gates, enter these courts of his, with hymns of praise, give him thanks, and bless his name. Gracious is the Lord, everlasting his mercy; age after age, he is faithful to his promise still." (99: 1, 2, 4, 5)

We eagerly *pass through these gates,* and enter with gladness *these courts of his,* where our Lord and Brother is offering adoration to his Father in our name. The most unworthy of us thus gains access to the Holy of Holies. There we participate in the only act of adoration which is perfect. The eucharistic sacrifice is the perfect act of adoration because Christ as man is adoring the Father by continually offering through his priests the sacrifice which he offered on the Cross. Through the real separation of his body and blood on the Cross, and the mystical separation of them in the Mass, he proclaims that God is the Lord and Master of life and death.

Every day we can say that *the whole earth keeps holiday in God's honor* because every day, in every part of the world, his true worshippers unite their adoration with that of his divine Son in the Mass. When it is our turn to pass through that gate of his, which is his Son, we have good reason to *appear in his presence with glad hearts.*

Life has many burdens, but there is none that weighs more heavily upon us than that of our transgressions against the law of our Father. All of us gathered around the altar of Christ's sacrifice have sinned. During Mass, we can look up with joyful relief because our High Priest is offering the perfect act of reparation for our sins of commission and omission.

We are reassured by the very words with which our Lord changes the wine into his precious blood: "for this is my blood, of the new testament, shed for many, to the remission of sin." Writing of the sacrifice which Christ offered on the Cross to redeem us from sin, Pius XII observed: ". . . on Calvary Christ built a font of purification and salvation which he filled with the blood he shed; but if men do not bathe in it and there wash away their iniquities, they can never be purified and saved. . . . The august Sacrifice of the altar is, as it were, the supreme instrument whereby the merits won by the divine Redeemer upon the Cross are distributed to the faithful; as often as this commemorative Sacrifice is offered, there is wrought the work of our Redemption." At every Mass, we can sing with the psalmist: *Gracious is the Lord, everlasting his mercy.* The cleansing stream of Christ's blood flows anew during the Mass, washing away the sins of those who truly unite with the supreme Priest as he offers the perfect act of atonement in their name.

Our joy in the Mass is further increased because it fulfills the third purpose of worship, the offering of supplication to God. The Mass is the perfect act of petition, as Pope Pius XII explains: ". . . Christ is a priest; but he is a priest not for himself but for us, when in the name of the whole human race he offers our prayers and religious homage to the eternal Father. . . ."

Doubt that our prayers will be heard is not based on any questioning of our Lord's direct promise, *Ask, and you shall receive,* but on our own unworthiness. We are indeed unworthy, but Christ is praying with us, and for us, particularly in the Mass, and he is always heard. When we unite ourselves with the sacrifice of Christ in the Mass, offering our petitions while he is offering himself in sacrifice, he makes our prayers his own.

To reassure us that our Lord is offering our prayers to his Father, the Church ends many of the prayers of the Mass with the powerful and beautiful phrase: *through Jesus Christ, thy Son, our Lord.* Again we make our own the words of the psalm: *He is faithful to his promise still.*

Finally, there is our joy in having the Mass as the perfect act of thanksgiving. The very word, *Eucharist,* means to offer thanks. The offering of thanks is a matter of obligation. We *owe* God thanks for all the benefits he has bestowed upon us, benefits of both soul and body. In the eucharistic sacrifice, Christ is thanking his Father in our name. The Church reminds us of this by having the server, or the congregation, respond to the words of the priest, from time to time during the Mass: *Deo gratias.* Thus, in the phrase of the psalm, *we give him thanks and bless his name.*

Streams of joy are waiting to be released through this perfect act of sacrifice. The joy that priests and people actually receive through the Mass is proportionate to their understanding of the role that they play in offering Christ's oblation. They share in the fruits of the sacrifice only to the extent that they participate in their daily lives in the Passion and Cross, of which the Mass is the living memorial. This is what St. Peter had in mind when he wrote to the whole Church: ". . . you must be a holy priesthood, to offer up that spiritual sacrifice which God accepts through Jesus Christ" (I Pet. 2:5).

St. Paul joins St. Peter in stressing the necessity of true union with Christ's sacrifice: "And now, brethren, I appeal to you by God's mercies to offer up your bodies as a living sacrifice, consecrated to God and worthy of his acceptance; this is the worship due from you as rational creatures" (Rom. 12:1). The joy that comes to us through the Mass depends to a great extent on the effort we make to release the incalculable divine energy that is potentially ours through the action of our divine Priest.

The Mass can hardly produce its effects in us if we think of it as something separate from our daily life. We turn away after Mass, not as from something finished, but as from something begun. If we have assisted at Mass with the proper attitude, we have offered ourselves, everything we have, and everything we do, in union with our High Priest. If the power of the Mass, and the joy of it, are to perdure, we have to continue offering ourselves in all the varied actions of our day.

Nothing that concerns us should remain apart from the sacrifice which we offer together with Christ in the Mass. Our work, whether pleasant or tedious, successful or unsuccessful, should be surrounded by the radiance of the Mass. Our recreations, our taking nourishment, our sleep, all our social relations, should be affected by the Mass.

If this becomes our way of acting, we return to Mass as though we had never left it. We begin to understand the rich significance of such a prayer as one found in the Mass of the feast of St. Paul of the Cross: *May these mysteries of thy passion and death, O Lord, confer on us that heavenly fervor with which St. Paul, while he offered them, presented his body as a living sacrifice, holy and pleasing to thee.*

18. The Joy of Holy Communion

The threefold joy that is ours in Holy Communion flows from the threefold effect of this greatest of the sacraments. The first effect of the Holy Eucharist is to keep us alive spiritually. The second effect is to increase our spiritual energy and vitality. The third effect is to bring us spiritual delight in receiving our Lord and our God.

This triple spiritual joy may be compared with the threefold physical satisfaction that results from the taking of our daily bread. The first satisfaction that we have in food is that it preserves our physical life. However, we do not eat merely to stay alive, but to grow strong. And so the second satisfaction that comes from nourishing ourselves is that, through food, we increase our physical energy and vitality. The third satisfaction in taking nourishment is that it gratifies the sense of taste.

The psalmist praised the Creator for the gift of natural food when he sang: "Thy hand gives earth all her plenty. Grass must grow for the cattle; for man, too, she must put forth her shoots, if he is to bring corn out of her bosom; if there is to be wine that will rejoice man's heart, oil to make his face shine, and bread that will keep man's strength from failing." (Ps. 103:13-15)

Both in the promise of the Eucharist and in its institution Christ stresses his intention that this sacrament is to be our spiritual food and drink. In the promise of it, he said: "I myself am the living bread that has come down from heaven. If anyone eats of this bread, he shall live forever. And now, what is this bread which I am to give? It is my flesh, given for the life of the world. . . . My flesh is real food, my blood is real drink. He who eats my flesh, and drinks my blood, lives continually in me, and I in him." (Jn. 6:51-52, 56-57) And in the actual institution he said: "Take, *eat,* this is my body. . . . *Drink,* all of you, of this: for this is my blood." (Matt. 26:26-28; Lk. 22:19)

Just as the first effect of material food is to preserve physical life by warding off death, so the first effect of Holy Communion is to preserve the life of the soul by warding off mortal sin, which causes the death of the soul, as the very word *mortal* indicates. There is nothing more important than to convince sensual people that in the Holy Eucharist lies the cure of their debilitation. This salutary effect of Holy Communion is summed up by St. Cyril of Alexandria when he says: "For Christ, abiding in us, lulls to sleep the law of the flesh which rages in our members." St. Augustine says that "as charity grows, lust diminishes: when charity reaches perfection, lust is no more." These two doctors of the Church are not referring to lust only in the sense of carnal desire, but to lust in any form: lust for money and material goods, lust for honor and power.

The most basic joy in both the physical and spiritual order is based on the preservation of the precious thing we call *life*. In the supernatural order, preservation of life is impossible for anybody who knows of Holy Communion but who refuses this divine nutriment. Christ made this clear when he said: "Believe me when I tell you this: you can have no life in yourselves, unless you eat the flesh of the Son of Man, and drink his blood" (Jn. 6:54).

While there is a basic joy in preserving life, a person

would be regarded as eccentric if he ate only enough to keep himself alive. There are few things more obvious than the satisfaction that a healthy person receives from a hearty meal. He rises from table, as we say, bursting with energy and vitality. In a similar way, one who receives Holy Communion just to throw off the threat of grave sin will not experience the full joy of this sacrament. Authentic joy can come to the communicant only by having the spiritual energy and vitality that are stored up in this divine granary flow into his soul. It is a profound truth that the graces waiting to be released through Holy Communion are so vast that one Communion well received is capable of making a man or woman a saint. Limitless grace is there for the taking. The Holy Eucharist is truly the food of the strong, but only for those who want it to be so.

The measure of what we actually receive, and the joy of that measure, depend on our willingness to remove obstacles to the free flowing of the graces of Holy Communion. These obstacles are habitual venial sins—habitual acts of impatience, lying, unkindness, irreverence, injustice.

Just as the person who takes only enough nourishment to be able to toddle about deprives himself of the joy of vigorous living, so the believer in the Eucharist who fails to receive the sacrament often, or who fails to dispose himself properly for it, deprives himself of that peace and joy which are the reward of those who rightfully treat this gift of which it can be said, with St. Augustine: *God, in his infinite wisdom, knew not how to give more; God, in his infinite power, could not have given more; God, in his infinite riches, had not more to give.*

The third effect of food is to afford pleasure by the

satisfaction of the sense of taste. So great is this satisfaction that man has always used the joy of feasting as the most common expression of jubilation. Whatever the occasion for rejoicing—marriage, homecoming, the bestowal of some honor—the joy of the fiesta is symbolized by the festive board. We refer to Holy Communion as the Lord's Supper. But this supper is always a feast.

With a shout of joy, St. Thomas Aquinas, the poet of the Holy Eucharist, exclaims: *O sacred banquet, in which Christ is received, the memory of his Passion recalled, the mind is filled with grace, and a pledge of future glory is given to us.* It is our supreme joy to partake of this banquet. There are two aspects of our joy in it: nothing brings greater joy in itself than this sacrament. And there is no fitter way of expressing rejoicing on some occasion that has particular spiritual significance than by partaking of this banquet.

Added to this is the fact that a person's pleasure in eating is increased when he takes his food with those he loves, or with those who are his close associates. Such companionship serves as a very effective seasoning. Although in Communion every man communes alone with his God, we approach the table of the Lord together. This is especially appropriate since one of the primary purposes of Holy Communion is to create a bond, not only between a man and his God, but between man and man. It is for this reason that the Eucharist is called the sacrament of peace and unity.

The unity which the Holy Eucharist fosters is symbolized by the way in which the bread and wine that are used in the consecration have their unity from the coming together of a multitude of things. The bread, although one substance, is made up of many grains of wheat. The wine, while also one substance, has its unity from the confluent juices of many grapes. A great part of our joy in the Holy Eucharist comes from the peace and unity among brethren which flow from it.

A sense of realism demands that we recognize that we are spiritual parasites if our Holy Communions do not lead to greater communion with our fellowman. We have no right to the joy of receiving Christ if we leave his table without the determination to do what we can to bring this living bread to our spiritually famished brethren. If we were content to partake of this divine bread, never lifting a finger to share it with others, we would be more worthy of condemnation than Dives, for he denied Lazarus only material food.

The full joy of Holy Communion can be ours if we apply the doctrine of St. Paul: "Is not the bread we break a participation in Christ's body? The one bread makes us one body, though we are many in number; the same bread is shared by all." (I Cor. 10:16-17) The Apostle is saying that the express purpose of Holy Communion is to make us one with Christ and all the members of his Mystical Body. If we are not really one in mind and heart, the purpose of our Lord in instituting the Holy Eucharist is defeated.

One test of whether we are united with Christ and our fellowman is our attitude toward others after leaving the table at which we have received him who gave us the perfect example of courtesy, generosity, thoughtfulness and service. How much of his love and joy are left uncommunicated because those who receive him in Holy Communion descend the steps of his house, walk among his brethren as though they were complete strangers, and drive away without any thought of communicating with fellow-communicants? How easily we forget that Christ linked the Holy Eucharist with love and service of others by washing his disciples' feet at the first eucharistic supper.

The union of brethren, which is the secondary effect of Communion, influences the primary effect, union with God. The joy of this union is reflected in words associated with *communion: communicative, accessible, approachable, conversable, unconstrained, easy to speak to, outgoing*. Our God is all these things to us in Holy Communion, and much more.

Holy Communion rounds out the grace and gladness that are ours in the eucharistic sacrifice. This completion of the eucharistic mystery through Holy Communion is indicated by the prayer of the Canon of the Mass: *We most humbly beseech thee, Almighty God, . . . that as many of us as, by participation at this altar, shall receive the most sacred body and blood of thy Son, may be filled with every heavenly blessing and grace. Through the same Christ, our Lord.*

In his heart-to-heart talk with the disciples at the Last Supper, Jesus said: "I am the vine, you are its branches; if a man lives on in me, and I in him, then he will yield abundant fruit; separated from me, you have no power to do anything. . . . All this I have told you, so that my joy may be yours, and the measure of your joy may be filled up." (Jn. 15:5, 11)

In an encyclical which is rich in doctrine and eloquence, Pope Leo XIII reflected the joy of all of us in the Holy Eucharist. "This Sacrament," he wrote, "is, as it were, the very soul of the Church. From it the Church draws all her strength, all her glory, her every supernatural endowment and adornment, every good thing that is hers."

19. The Joy of Our Lady

One of the best ways of appreciating something we value is to lose it, or to imagine what it would mean to lose it. The best way to appreciate fine weather is to have a spell of stormy or cloudy weather. We appreciate good health after we have been ill. A Catholic knows that he will never lose our Lady, but this does not prevent his imagining how much joy would be missing from his life if she were not part of it.

No Catholic could convey better the sense of loss which he would experience if Mary were not there to turn to in time of joy or in time of sorrow, in time of peace or in time of trouble, than is conveyed in the lines of one who for most of her life was deprived of a knowledge of the Mother of Christ. In a deeply moving poem, "Prayer to the Florence Madonna," Cornelia Otis Skinner bares her sense of loss thus:

> Mary, most serenely fair,
> Hear an unbeliever's prayer.
> Nurtured in an austere creed,
> Sweetest Lady, she has need
> Of the solace of your grace;
> See the tears that stain her face
> As she kneels to beg your love—
> You whom no one taught her of.[1]

[1] Reprinted with the permission of the author.

When a non-Catholic once observed that Catholics appear to be a happy people, a Catholic present replied that this was partly due to our having a mother in the Church. This book has been emphasizing that a Catholic has countless reasons for spiritual joy, but surely one of the greatest is possession of a mother in the spiritual order, and a mother of such peerless beauty, love and power.

Nothing would be more natural for a son or daughter whose mother was graced with physical beauty than to be proud of this quality in her. Mary's beauty is so great that for two thousand years Catholics have been trying to outdo each other in giving the world some idea of it.

The Catholic Church regards Mary as God's masterpiece. Of all purely human beings, she is the greatest. No artist ever lavished on painting or sculpture the care and attention that God lavished on her who was to be the mother of his divine Son. From the first moment he brought her into existence he prevented the blight of original sin from touching her, thus making her the only member of the human race, apart from him who is also God, to enter the world with a soul free from this stain. We may suppose that it was her joy in this exalted privilege that caused her to answer Bernadette's question as to her identity with the simple statement: "I am the Immaculate Conception."

Catholics rejoice that she is also the only simply human being who was entirely free from all actual sin. The human soul, when unstained by sin, is inexpressibly beautiful. Since Mary was without both original and actual sin, we can understand why the saints were as one in expressing their praise of her, praise which sounds exaggerated, and even blasphemous, to many non-Catholics.

The joy of the saints in extolling the Mother of God

accounts for what appears to be their extravagant use of language. Typical are the words of St. Louis de Montfort: "God has a most rich treasury in which he has laid up all that he has of beauty and splendor, of rareness and preciousness, even to his own Son, and this immense treasury is none other than Mary, whom the saints have called the Treasure of the Lord."

Another quotation, from an earlier writer, will perhaps indicate how common this high praise of Mary has been among Catholics. Hugh of St. Victor speaks to our Lady in this fashion: "Thou art all fair: thou art fair within, fair without; within in thy heart, without in thy body: within thou art ruddy, without thou art white: red by charity, white through chastity." Catholic writers have not been concerned that they will be too eloquent in lauding the Mother of Christ, but that they will not be eloquent enough.

If we are criticized for the prominence we give our Lady, our answer is that we have taken our cue from God, who placed her at the very center of the mystery of redemption by making her the virgin Mother of the Redeemer. If our praise of her is regarded as extreme, we reply that no praise of her has been greater than that contained in the salutation of the angel, who said to her, speaking in God's name: ". . . thou art full of grace" (Lk. 1:28).

The two parts of the Hail Mary express our reasons for joy in Mary. In the first part, we delight in addressing her in the words first used by the angel: "Hail, thou who art full of grace; the Lord is with thee; blessed art thou among women" (Lk. 1:28). In the phrase which ends this part of the prayer, "and blessed is the fruit of thy womb, Jesus," we sum up the angel's tribute to the Son that our Lady was to bear: "thou shalt conceive in thy womb, and shalt bear a son, and thou shalt call him Jesus. He shall be great, and men will know him for the Son of the most High. . . .; his kingdom shall never have an end." (Lk. 1:31-33)

We rejoice in that sinlessness which made her perfectly pleasing to God, and that her sinlessness prepared her for such spiritual adornment that she could be described as full of grace. We rejoice that we have received through her the Savior, Christ, our Lord and our Brother. We rejoice that he who said that he had received all power in heaven and on earth decreed, as Pius XII said in a broadcast to 700,000 pilgrims at Fatima, "for his heavenly Mother all glory, power and majesty of his Kingdom."

We cannot help experiencing a very special joy in the conviction that she who possesses limitless power with God, that she who has been presented "to the celestial court seated at the right hand of the immortal King of Ages," is not only the Mother of God, but ours also. (Pius XII, in aforementioned broadcast.) Here we have the reason for our joy in the second part of the Hail Mary. She who was given to us by our elder Brother on Calvary with the words "This is thy mother" is waiting to use her tremendous power in our behalf. No mother has ever been so eager to obtain favors for her children.

Of this mother of ours, St. Alphonsus says that she is "the dispenser of all graces." "Every grace that is communicated to the world," says St. Bernadine of Siena, "has a threefold origin: it flows from God to Christ, from Christ to the Virgin, from the Virgin to us."

If we are accused of ascribing too much power to her, we can reply that it was her divine Son who first intimated that she would be refused nothing that she asked. When he changed the water into wine at the wedding feast of

Cana, he did it because of a mere hint from her. And this was after he had told her that his time for manifesting his divinity through public miracles had not arrived.

The significance of this miracle is understood more clearly when we think of the apparent unimportance of the occasion. It did not seem a world-shaking tragedy that this bridegroom was embarrassed because the wine had run out at his wedding reception. The guests had already had their fill, as is indicated by the surprise of the master of the feast that the better wine should have been served last. "It is ever the good wine that men set out first," he said to the bridegroom, "and the worse kind only when all have drunk deep; thou hast kept the good wine until now" (Jn. 2:10).

We cannot fail to be impressed by our Lady's assured manner when she said to the servants at the wedding feast, "Do whatever he tells you," and this after he appeared to be refusing her implied request by telling her that his time had not come for working public miracles (Jn. 2:5). If such was her power while still herself a pilgrim to eternity, it will be understood that this power has reached its full development in her role as Queen of the Universe.

A marriage reception is almost invariably a happy occasion. But no marriage has shed such a radiant joy, not only on the guests, but on those who have merely heard about it. The warmth of Mary's maternal concern for the newlyweds and their guests is a quality that we also have felt. The joy of that occasion is renewed every time she exercises her power in our favor. It is as though we were attending innumerable feasts, with Mary shedding over them a joy whose color and tone are identified with her, a color and tone whose beauty and melody have a strictly Marian quality.

We may compare the apparitions that she has made from time to time with a wedding feast, a constantly renewed feast celebrating the marriage of her divine Son with the Church, his spouse. Such apparitions are an invitation to participate even while in this world in the joy of the eternal feast. Anyone who has been at Guadalupe, Lourdes, or any other of the shrines which celebrate appearances of our Lady, feels a joy which is almost tangible.

Whether she is appearing to a middle-aged man like Juan Diego at Guadalupe, or to a young girl like Bernadette at Lourdes, she appears because she wants us to understand how close she is to all of us. In speaking to them she speaks to us. She does not often appear visibly, because in this life we walk mainly by faith. Whether she appears to our senses or not, she is always making her presence felt by those who listen to the words the Church applies to her in Masses of her feasts: "It is I that give birth to all noble loving, all reverence, all true knowledge, and the holy gift of hope. From me comes every grace of faithful observance, from me all promise of life and vigor. Hither turn your steps, all you that have learned to long for me; take your fill of the increase I yield. Never was honey so sweet as the influence I inspire, never honeycomb as the gift I bring; mine is a renown that endures, age after age. Eat of this fruit, and you will yet hunger for more; drink of this wine, and your thirst for it is still unquenched. He who listens to me will never be disappointed; he who lives by me will do no wrong; he who reads my lesson aright will find in it life eternal." (Ecclus. 24:24-31)

We have only the faintest idea now of the joy that we will have when we find her waiting to welcome us on the shores of eternity. Then we will fully realize the depths of meaning in the title with which we address her even in this world: *Cause of Our Joy*. Enjoying with her the Vision of the Triune God, we will understand the seeds of joy contained in her exultant *Magnificat*: "My soul magnifies the Lord; my spirit has found joy in God, who is my Savior, because he has looked graciously upon the lowliness of his handmaid. Behold, from this day forward all generations will count me blessed; because he who is mighty, he whose name is holy, has wrought for me his wonders." (Lk.1:46-49)

20. The Joy of Our Angels

One of the most exciting truths of our faith is strangely neglected. We find fascination in the question whether there are intelligent beings on other planets. Supposing there are such beings, we may never discover their existence. There are, however, intelligent beings, other than men, whose existence every believer acknowledges, and then proceeds pretty much to ignore. Every one of us has his own angel, who acts as companion, counselor, guardian, consoler and intercessor, and generally we not only pay no heed to his influence on our lives, but usually disregard his very presence.

We do not have to feel a deep guilt if we have failed to give our angel the attention that he deserves. There is some excuse for our neglect in the fact that we have never seen, or heard, our angel, or felt his presence in any other sensible way. But we should realize that we are depriving ourselves of a substantial joy by not adverting to our having at our side all during our earthly pilgrimage such a powerful and charming friend as our guardian angel.

The presence of our angel prevents our ever being alone. Ordinarily, we do not enjoy being by ourselves, or doing things alone. At least, this is true of those who are not called to the solitude of monastic or conventual life. Few people like to recreate alone. We are inclined to feel a little sorry when we see somebody eating alone. The loneliness that results when a person has to live alone is regarded as one of life's greatest crosses. Lonely people should wake up and realize that there would be a lot more joy in their lives if they were more conscious of the constant companionship of their guardian angel.

It is true, of course, that we would not be alone if we did not have the companionship of our angel, because God is present to us every moment of our existence. But God himself made clear the advantages in man's having other intelligent beings than himself as companions. As he prepared to create Eve, God said: "It is not well that man should be without companionship" (Gen. 2:18). The same beneficent Creator decided that man should also have the companionship of an angel.

That each of us has his individual angel is indicated by the words of our Lord. After calling a child to his side, he said: "See to it that you do not treat one of these little ones with contempt; I tell you, *they have angels of their own in heaven, that behold the face of my heavenly Father continually*" (Matt. 18:10).

Before considering the services rendered so gladly by

our guardian angels, it will be helpful to look at the angels in general. Angels are mentioned in practically all the Books of the Old and New Testaments. The important part that the angels play in the destiny of human beings is revealed by the most cursory reading of Holy Scripture.

The angels differ in rank and power. St. Thomas, following St. Denis, divides the angels into three hierarchies, each of which contains three orders. Their proximity to the Supreme Being serves as the basis for this division. In the first order, St. Thomas placed the Seraphim, Cherubim and Thrones. In the second order, the Dominions, Virtues and Powers. And in the third, the Principalities, Archangels and Angels. Even the Angelic Doctor, however, was not certain of the exact offices performed by the different orders of angels. This is shown by his writing: "the guardianship of the human race belongs to the order of *Principalities,* or *perhaps* to the Archangels, whom we call the princes. Hence, Michael, whom we call an *Archangel,* is also called *one of the princes.*"

We do not have to know the offices of the various orders of angels in order to echo their joy in praising God. The Church has us join our song to theirs in the *preface* of the Mass, the joyous hymn of thanksgiving which opens the *canon* of the Holy Sacrifice. In the preface which is used in most of the Masses throughout the liturgical year, we find ourselves uniting with the choirs of angels in exultation, as we sing: *It is truly meet and just, right and availing to salvation, that we should at all times, and in all places, give thanks unto thee, O holy Lord, Father Almighty and everlasting God, through Christ our Lord. Through whom the Angels praise thy majesty, the Dominions worship it, the Powers stand in awe. The heavens, and the heavenly hosts, and the blessed Seraphim, join to-*

gether in celebrating their joy. With whom we pray thee join our voices also, while we say with lowly praise: Holy, holy, holy, Lord God of hosts. Heaven and earth are full of thy glory. Hosanna in the highest.

There are only three angels whose names we know, Michael, Gabriel and Raphael. As St. Thomas indicated, they appear to be, with the other Archangels, the guardian angels of the whole human race. Evidently, every country has a guardian angel. This idea is based on the statement of the Archangel Gabriel to the prophet Daniel: "And now I will return to fight against the prince of the Persians. . . . And none is my helper in all these things but Michael, who is guardian of your race." (Dan. 10:20, 21) St. Thomas holds that if a man's office in society is of unusual importance, he may have more than one guardian angel.

The high rank and power of Michael are shown also in the Apocalypse, where he is described as leader of the angelic hosts in the battle against Lucifer and his cohorts: "Fierce war broke out in heaven, where Michael and his angels fought against the dragon . . . the great dragon, serpent of the primal age, was flung down to earth; he whom we call the devil, or Satan, the whole world's seducer, flung down to earth, and his angels with him." (Apoc. 12:7-9) The Church emphasizes the importance of Michael's relationship to us by making his feast, September 29, of the rank of first class. The feasts of Gabriel and Raphael are of third-class rank. Michael is much closer to all of us than we realize.

While Michael emerges as the great heavenly warrior, Gabriel appears as the messenger of joy. We find him discussing with the prophet Daniel the most joyous event in the history of mankind, the coming of the long-awaited

Messias. It was he also who appeared to the priest, Zachary, as he offered incense in the sanctuary, and told him that his wife, Elizabeth, Mary's cousin, would soon bear him his first child, although they "both were now well advanced in years." "Joy and gladness shall be thine," said Gabriel, referring to the birth of John the Baptist, "and many hearts shall rejoice over his birth, for he is to be high in the Lord's favor. . . . My name is Gabriel, and my place is in God's presence; I have been sent to speak with thee, and to bring thee this good news." (Lk. 1:8, 14, 19)

It was Gabriel again who was the bearer of the gladdest news of all, when he appeared to Mary, within six months of Elizabeth's conceiving, and told her that she was to give birth to the Son of God. It is a traditional belief that it was likewise Gabriel who announced to the overjoyed shepherds that the Savior had been born. It is generally thought that Gabriel was the angel who appeared to comfort our Lord toward the end of his agony in Gethsemani.

Raphael is regarded as the angel of health and healing because he restored the sight of the elder Tobias, after four years of blindness, and also delivered the bride of the younger Tobias from the power of the devil. Nowhere will we find a better illustration of the joy of man's relationship to the angels than in the Book of Tobias. We read there how the Archangel Raphael made himself the companion of young Tobias on a journey that Tobias was making at his father's request. Raphael saved the young man from being injured by a huge fish that lunged at him as he washed his feet in a river, helped him choose a wife, collected a debt that was owed to his father, and did so many other favors for them that father and son, taking him for a human being, wanted to give him half their possessions.

Great light is thrown on the way the angels deal with man by the statement which Raphael made to the two Tobiases as he was about to take leave of them. Calling them aside, he said: "Come, let me tell you the whole truth of the matter. . . . When thou, Tobias, wert praying, . . . when thou wert burying the dead, leaving thy dinner untasted . . . I, all the while, was offering that prayer of thine to the Lord. Then, because thou hadst found favor, needs must that trials should come, and test thy worth. And now, for thy healing, for the deliverance of thy son's wife, Sara, from the fiend's attack, he has chosen me for his messenger. Who am I? I am the angel Raphael, and my place is among those seven who stand in the presence of the Lord." (Tob. 12:11-15)

Such stories as that of Tobias are recorded in Holy Scripture for our instruction and encouragement. Raphael and the other angels are waiting to bring into our lives the joy that was brought to the family of Tobias. The only requirement is that we live as prayerfully and uprightly as they did.

It is safe to say that God had angels appear outwardly more often under the Old Testament than under the New because, before the coming of Christ, the People of God were in greater need than we are of reassurance regarding the constant presence of the unseen God and the closeness of the invisible world. God has appeared visibly in Christ, and Christ will be present to the Church until the end of time, as he declared to the Apostles a moment before his ascension: "And behold I am with you all through the days that are coming, until the consummation of the world" (Matt. 28:20). Since his coming, the angels have continued their ministry to men, but have more rarely made their presence known through visible manifestations.

Angels were forever appearing to men like Abraham, Isaac, Jacob, Moses, Elias and the other prophets. We do not find them appearing with the same frequency, for instance, to the Apostles. Such an experience as Philip had when he was directed by an angel to meet the chariot of the Ethiopian courtier at a crossroads was exceptional. The same can be said of the appearance to Peter of the angel who led him through the corridors of Herod's prison to safety outside.

That the first members of the Church were quite conscious of the ministry of the angels is shown in a diverting sequel to Peter's liberation. Once outside the prison, he decided to make his way to the house of the mother of a disciple named John, also called Mark. We read in the Acts: "Here many had gathered for prayer; a girl named Rhoda came to answer, when he knocked at the porch door, and she, recognizing Peter's voice, was too overjoyed to open the gate for him; she ran in, and told them that Peter was standing at the gate. Thou art mad, they told her, but she still insisted that it was so; and then they said, *It must be his guardian angel.* Meanwhile, Peter went on knocking; so they opened, and found him there, and stood astonished." (Acts 12:7-16)

Some of the later saints were favored with appearances of their guardian angels, but such instances are infrequent. St. Frances of Rome, who died as a widow in 1440, after founding a religious house for women, often saw and spoke with her angel. The Church makes note of this in the collect of her feast, March 9: *O God, who among other gifts of thy grace, didst honor thy servant Frances by frequent colloquies with her angel, we ask thee to grant, through her help, that we also may enjoy the fellowship of angels. Through Jesus Christ, thy Son, our Lord.*

Another saint who frequently saw and conversed with her guardian angel was St. Gemma Galgani, who died as recently as 1903, at the age of twenty-five. She talked with her angel with as much ease as with relatives and friends. Her confessor and director, Father Germano, a Passionist of wide scientific knowledge and great intellectual acumen, testified to the many extraordinary supernatural phenomena in St. Gemma's life. One of these preternatural occurrences was the sending of letters to Father Germano through the ministry of St. Gemma's angel.

For some years before she was given the privilege of seeing and talking with her guardian angel, Gemma had made a practice on entering a church of offering a few prayers in honor of her angel. It is not unlikely that this early attention to her spiritual guardian won for her the grace of having her angel manifest himself visibly.

When we give thought to our guardian angel, we first think of him as a companion. We would regard it as rude if we ignored the presence of a person with whom we set out on a journey. Unfortunately, this is the way we act toward the angel who accompanies us on our journey to heaven. When God appointed an angel to go before the chosen people as they wandered through the desert on their way to the promised land, he said, "And now I am sending my angel to go before thee and guard thee on thy way, and lead thee to the place I have made ready for thee. Give him good heed, and listen to his bidding; think not to treat him with neglect" (Ex. 23:20, 21). God says the same to us with regard to our individual guardian angel. St. Bernard reminds us that the first obligation we have toward our angel is "reverence for his presence." We can hardly show him reverence if we do not advert to his being at our side. Pope Pius XI also placed reverence first in speaking of our relationship to our angel. The Pontiff observed: "The conviction that we are protected by a prince of the heavenly army, by one of those chosen spirits of whom Christ said that they always see the face of God—this conviction fills us with reverence, devotion, and firm confidence."

In our guardian angel, we also have a counselor whose wisdom and knowledge surpass that of the wisest and most learned man on earth. St. Thomas dwells on this aspect of the ministry of our angel when he says: "Guardianship is ordained to illumination by instruction, as to its ultimate and principal effect." Not everyone is called to the type of austerity that characterized the life of St. Gemma, who was so conformed to the crucified Christ that she received the stigmata. The counsel that she received from her angel would hardly be applicable to persons who have not achieved her degree of sanctity.

The following advice given to Gemma by her guardian angel is quoted, not because it would apply to the ordinary reader, but to show that our angel is always ready to offer us counsel appropriate to our state. The first occasion that Gemma saw her guardian angel was when she was attending a reception in the bishop's house on the day of her graduation. She was wearing a gold necklace and medal, an award for having been first in her class scholastically. Her angel looked at her sharply, and said: "The jewelry of a bride of our crucified King is to be only thorns and the cross." Later, he was to counsel her regarding her prayer, spurring her on to greater fervor. That it was not all severity is evident from his willingness to act as messenger to her spiritual director.

Most of us probably think of the title, guardian angel, as implying that our angel guards us from physical harm. That this is one of his ministrations is borne out by the words of the psalm: "He has given charge to his angels concerning thee, to watch over thee wheresoever thou goest; they will hold thee up with their hands lest thou shouldst chance to trip on a stone" (Ps. 90:11, 12). Only in heaven will we know how many times we have been saved from accident, or death, through the intervention of our angel. In order to rejoice in our guardian angel's protection, we do not have to know how many times he has shielded us from harm, but only that this is one of his offices toward us.

No friend on earth is more ready to console us in those hours of grief and trouble that come to all of us than our angel. He is at our side in times of difficulty, disturbance, and apparent frustration. He is with us in temptation. He is present when everything seems to be dark and discouraging.

Finally, our angel acts as our intercessor before the throne of God, where he eternally assists, even while acting as our guardian in this world. That the angels offer our prayers to God is evident from many parts of Holy Scripture, particularly the Apocalypse, where the incense that they are described as offering is a symbol of the prayers of God's servants on earth. As the Archangel Raphael said to Tobias, "I, all the while, was offering that prayer of thine to the Lord" (Tob. 12:12).

St. Denis said that the angels are "the brightest mirrors of divinity." It is for us to decide whether these exalted personages, who are, at the same time, assistants at the throne of God and our companions and guardians on earth, will bring into our lives the joy that can be ours by a proper consciousness and evaluation of their ministry.

21. The Joy of Action

The Creator has made us in such fashion that we delight in action. The joy that comes to living beings through the exercise of their vital powers could not be more obvious. Whether the vital power that we are exercising at a given moment be physical, mental, or spiritual, we find satisfaction in its exercise. A child will go through the simple motion of throwing a stone into a pond, and watch with contentment the spreading ripples that result from his action. An artist will stand back and regard with pleasure the picture that has sprung from the action of his brain and hand. A publisher, or an editor, will walk through a train and notice with contentment how many people appear absorbed by the newspaper that is produced by the action of his mind and imagination.

So great is our satisfaction in action that we are often fascinated by the action of other people. There are few things which bring more enjoyment than watching the graceful motions of expert skiers and skaters. Hundreds of thousands of people are regularly engrossed by the action of others as displayed in varied sports events, plays, motion pictures and television programs.

Philosophers say that God is *pure act,* and it is not surprising that he has placed in living creatures an overwhelming desire for action. Every living being contains its own spring of action. If it is balked in exercising the action of which it is capable, it instinctively fights to regain its freedom. An ineptly swatted fly strives desperately to regain the use of its legs and wings. It wants to get into action again.

Frustration is such an unpleasant experience because it means that some action which we have set in motion, or which we would like to set in motion, is impeded. There is a great deal of frustration in human lives. Sometimes people bring frustration on themselves, and at other times it is thrust upon them. A person who is imprisoned unjustly is frustrated physically through no fault of his. On the other hand, someone who moves to the suburbs, only to be plagued with boredom instead of enjoying the dream-life that he had expected, may have to ascribe his sense of boredom to his misjudgment. The same is true of retirement. The man who feels frustrated after enforced retirement may be able to blame the policy of the company that made him retire. But the person who voluntarily retires because he wants to do nothing for the rest of his life has only himself to blame for the ennui which is liable to result.

Boredom is mental weariness that comes from a lack of occupation or interest. We cannot help being bored by a flat speech, or the incessant talk of a garrulous person because we have no interest in what is being said. But we can help the ennui which accompanies voluntary inaction.

We were made for action, and the action in which we most often engage is the work through which we make our contribution to the welfare of mankind. There are few defects of character which earn more contempt than a failure to work. The very word *laziness* creates an image of irresponsibility. Goethe wrote about the curse that nature lays on those who flout her law of action and work. Boswell observed that it was better not to be than to be lazy, because if one did not exist, one had no harm in him, but that it was impossible to be lazy without being corrupt.

The words of St. Paul condemning laziness could hardly be stronger. He simply wrote that "the man who refuses to work must be left to starve" (II Thess. 3:10). Nobody in the history of the Church was in a better position to make such a statement than this man, whose work load, as he could boast, was greater than that of any of the other Apostles. He established churches all over the Roman Empire, preached everywhere, wrote long epistles. His travels, especially when one considers the means of transportation, would have brought physical exhaustion to any less willing worker. Unbelievably, along with his seemingly endless labors as an apostle, he carried on his former work as a tentmaker. It was to this latter work that he referred when he wrote to the Thessalonians: "We would not even be indebted to you for our daily bread, we earned it in weariness and toil, working with our hands, night and day, so as not to be a burden to any of you; not that we are obliged to do so, but as a model for your own behavior . . ." (II Thess. 3:8-9).

That joy accompanied his labors, particularly those in which he engaged for the spread of Christ's kingdom, is evident from the way in which such words as *joy* and *rejoice* are scattered through his epistles. To the Thessalonians, to whom he had complained about the weariness and toil that accompanied his manual labor, he wrote: "Joy be with you always" (I Thess. 5:16). It was immediately after he had mentioned to the Philippians those who had shared "the yoke so loyally . . . worked for the gospel at my side, as much as Clement and those other fellow laborers of mine," that he struck the note of exultation which reechoes through the Church at the opening of the Mass of Gaudete Sunday every year: "Joy to you in the Lord at all times; once again I wish you joy" (Phil. 4:4). It was also to the Philippians that he said: "I joy and rejoice with you" (2:17, CV).

It is in the work of extending the Kingdom of Christ that we Christians should mainly seek the joy of action. We have no right, as rational beings, to rejoice in action which is not intelligent. Intelligent action is that which leads to the fulfillment of God's purpose in our regard, and that of our fellowman. God's purpose is chiefly that men come to know him and the Son whom he sent into the world. One billion of the three billion people on earth know and acknowledge him, and this gives some basis for rejoicing, but we have no reason to stop working as long as a single human being remains untouched by the influence of Christ, our Lord.

If there is joy in work, it is mainly the result of a feeling of accomplishment. This is usually what a person has in mind when he says that he enjoys his work. There could be no greater accomplishment for one who believes in God than to be instrumental in bringing his life to other men. In that dramatic encounter in which Jesus, with such ease, persuaded two sets of brothers to drop their fishing nets and follow him, we sense his human and divine magnetism. But we should also note the attractive challenge contained in the type of work he was offering them in exchange for their occupation as fishermen. Christ merely said: "Come and follow me; *I will make you into fishers of men*" (Matt. 4:20). At the same moment Jesus approached, Peter and his brother Andrew were casting a net into the sea. St. Matthew says "they dropped their nets and left their father immediately, and followed him" (4:22). Precisely the same thing happened, moments later, with the sons of Zebedee, James and John.

Changing the analogy, Jesus observed, at the time he appointed the seventy-two disciples to aid in the work of preaching the word, that "the harvest is plentiful enough, but the laborers are few," and that they "must ask the Lord to whom the harvest belongs to send laborers out for the harvesting" (Lk. 10:2). Never have such vast fields been ready for harvesting as today. Never has the Church been in a better position to use spiritual laborers of every class, rank and age. Pope John XXIII made note of this great opportunity when he wrote: "Although it must be admitted that the times in which we live are torn by increasingly serious errors, and are troubled by violent disturbances, yet, it happens that the Church's laborers in this age have access to enormous fields of apostolic endeavor. This inspires us with uncommon hope." (*Mater et Magistra,* 260)

Pope John emphasized the opportunity that everybody has of making his ordinary and regular work serve the Church's apostolate. He wrote that "if Christians are also joined in mind and heart with the most holy Redeemer, when they apply themselves to temporal affairs, their work in a way is a continuation of the labor of Jesus Christ himself, drawing from it strength and redemptive power. 'He who abides in me, and I in him, he bears much fruit' (Jn. 15:5). Human labor of this kind is so exalted and ennobled that it leads men engaged in it to spiritual perfection, and can likewise contribute to the diffusion and propagation of the fruits of the Redemption to others. So also it results in the flow of that Gospel leaven, as it were, through the veins of civil society wherein we live and work." (*Ibid.,* 259)

Like St. Paul, Pope John, because of his example of industriousness, was in an unusually fine position to call others to a life of labor and effort. There was a divine irony in the contrast between the prognostications that his would be a stopgap reign, during which the Church would mark time, and those four and a half years that changed the face of the Church, and also left their mark on millions outside it.

Not being satisfied with such historic works as increasing the membership of the College of Cardinals, the convening of the first ecumenical council in almost a century, the publication of the monumental social encyclical, *Mater et Magistra,* and a stream of other writings and pronouncements, Pope John worked well into the eleventh hour, giving the world another great social encyclical, *Pacem in Terris,* in which he revealed his willingness to continue laboring over the smallest details of the political, economic and social program which the Church has so solicitously pieced together during the past three quarters of a century.

Pope Paul VI, as cardinal-archbishop of Milan, wrote prophetically: "The Church is entering a dynamic phase in her history, her whole organism is being set in motion in order to increase her apostolic efficiency. This immense effort, far from exhausting the Mystical Body of Christ, reinvigorates it, rejuvenates it, and causes it to flower anew. But the effort must be tremendous and complete: it covers the whole of the Church's traditional heritage of institutions which work under her jurisdiction; it attempts to rouse them, to make them reflect on their function, to make them consider the real end for which they were created; it reforms and modernizes them and gives them efficiency." These words could have been a comment on the Second Vatican Council. Actually, they were written in 1955, in a preface to Cardinal Suenens's book, *The Gospel to Every Creature,*[1] three years before the election of Pope John XXIII and eight years before the election of Pope Paul VI, when nobody seemed to be even remotely thinking of an ecumenical council.

The joy that participation in the work of the Council brought to the Council Fathers was reflected in their faces. The work was tiresome, but the burgeoning fruits that were the reward of their labor gladdened, not only the bishops themselves, but countless persons whose lives were affected for the better by the Council's deliberations, and by the very fact that the Council was held. While Pope Paul referred to the period following his elevation to the Chair of the Fisherman as "these toilsome days," especially since they were days filled with strenuous preparation for the reconvening of the Council, it was evident that he found joy in his work.

Pope and bishops have given priests and people an example of work and the joy to be found in it. The joy of implementation of the vigorous efforts of the prelates is left to the lower clergy, religious, and the laity. Priests have indicated that they are eager to second the work of their bishops. Before the Council, many of them had the joy of seeing their people participating, because of their own efforts, in the liturgy to a degree that would have been undreamed of a few decades ago. New currents of life have been flowing into religious orders, and their members have experienced fresh joy in a more energetic apostolate.

In our day, the laity particularly are being summoned to contribute their mighty energies to the work of the Church. It would be a tragedy if the *People of God* were to fail to hear the voices of the popes and bishops, who

[1] Westminster, Newman, 1957.

have been calling them so urgently to participation in the work of the hierarchy.

Pope Paul, in the preface to Cardinal Suenens's book referred to above, described the appeal which the Church has been making to the laity in recent years: "But the greatest and most remarkable effort is being put forward today by those members of the Church who, in past times, were passive rather than active, namely, the laity. And this is the new note that is struck: the laity are also called upon to collaborate in the work of the apostolate; the command of the Popes of our age, the cry of modern saints, the voice of the lay forerunners and guides of this great movement, like a powerful force penetrate the Christian body, still sound but inert: they lift it up, disturb it, in order to transform it. Is not every Christian a soldier of Christ? The hour for positive action has sounded; what is to be thought of anyone who would linger, passive and sluggish, deploring the evils of our day, and taking pleasure in criticizing those of their brothers who show a more generous goodwill than they do?"

Realist that he was, Pope John urged that the social doctrine of the Church "be included among the religious materials used to instruct and inspire the lay apostolate. . . ." "Let this diffusion of knowledge be accomplished," he wrote, "by every modern means: that is, in journals, whether daily or periodical; in doctrinal books, both for the learned and the general reader; and finally, by means of radio and television." (*Mater et Magistra,* 223)

"We judge that our sons among the laity," Pope John continued, "have much to contribute through their work and effort, that this teaching of the Catholic Church regarding the social question be more and more widely diffused. This they can do, not merely by learning it themselves and governing their actions accordingly, but also by taking special care that others also come to know its relevance. Let them be fully persuaded that in no better way can they show this teaching to be correct and effective, than by demonstrating that present-day social difficulties will yield to its application." (*Ibid.*, 224-5)

The three popes who bore the name of Pius in the present century were supremely conscious of the great need the Church has for lay participation in the work of her apostolate. St. Pius X sounded out a group of cardinals with the question: "What is the most necessary thing today for the salvation of society?" When he received such answers as more schools, more churches, more priests, he replied: "No, the prime necessity today is to have in every parish a group of laymen, virtuous, enlightened, resolute, fearless and truly apostolic." Pope Pius XI expressed the same idea in a trenchant phrase which has been widely quoted, but not widely enough applied: "The first apostles of the workers will be workers themselves." Pope Pius XII, with great practicality, stated: "the apostolate must be exercised in factories, in schools, in large apartment houses, not only by one's presence, but also by one's actions."

More of the laity would have acted on the stirring appeals of the popes during this century if priests and instructors had organized work for laymen on local levels, and if the laity had been shown the spiritual joy of working in the Master's vineyard.

The schema for the lay apostolate drawn up for the Second Vatican Council gives the layman a better idea of the work laid out for him by outlining three fields of action. The first is the field of social action. This comes down to the pressing duty of every human being to help make the world a better place in which to live. In this field, the layman has particular obligations. Catholic physicians, lawyers, scientists, merchants, businessmen, salesmen, laborers, journalists, move daily among other Christians, and among unbelievers, in the same fields of action. They have opportunities of bringing Christ, his teaching, and his life, to others that the priest never has. In influencing his environment, the layman needs no special invitation, and perhaps little direction. His warrant for action is his baptism. The only other things he needs are elevated motives and a knowledge of the principles of his faith.

The second field considered in the schema is that of Catholic organizations. This can be a very fruitful field, and one that is accompanied by its own kind of joy, because in it, one is working in concert with others. Anybody who has witnessed the effects of Catholic Action groups, of such organizations as the Legion of Mary, understands what can be accomplished when men and women band together for group effort in the cause of Christ.

The third field for lay action is the canonical mission of the Church to convert the world. In a general sense, this mission is given to all Christians through baptism, but its direction remains with the hierarchy. Whether an individual, or a family, joins the Papal Volunteers and goes to a foreign country in order to assist in the work of spreading the faith, or engages in such missionary work as street-corner speaking or convert instruction at home, any work of this kind is a sharing of the commission given to the Church to preach the Gospel to every creature.

Not only does the member of the Church who shirks his share in the work of the Church forego the joy that results from service, but he brings upon himself the condemnation of the Lord, who told such a stern parable about the use, or lack of use, of talents. Our divine Savior had the master of the servant who had buried his only talent reject with scorn the excuse of the servant that he had put it in a hole in the ground because his master was an exacting man.

Stressing human action in such a way that the divine action behind it is played down is to be guilty of activism. Pope John, after making a special appeal to the laity in *Mater et Magistra,* remarks that "in their dealings with men, they are bound to exert effort in such a way that while fulfilling their duties to others, they do so in union with God through Christ, for the increase of God's glory. Thus the Apostle Paul asserts: 'Whether you eat or drink, or do anything else, do all for the glory of God.' " Pursuing the same idea in *Pacem in Terris,* he observes: "Every believer in this world must be a spark of light, a center of love, a vivifying leaven amidst his fellowmen. And he will be this all the more perfectly the more closely he lives in communion with God in the intimacy of his own soul." (261)

22. *The Joy of Heaven*

In the Creed we profess our belief in the life of the world to come. It is a well-known fact, however, that very few believers are eager to leave the visible world for the invisible. On first consideration, a sort of practical agnosticism would appear to be at the bottom of this attitude, but such an explanation would be an oversimplification of the question. Another factor in the lack of eagerness to move from time to eternity is that the average person is not sure of what sort of a reception he deserves when he arrives before the judgment seat.

Heaven does not appear to be the subject of many sermons, and it is doubtful that it is often the subject of meditation. As a result, we deprive ourselves of the encouragement and inspiration that the thought of heaven would give us. We cheat ourselves of the joy of anticipating the peace, happiness and glory that await us when our earthly struggle is over.

The joy of anticipation is based on certain things we know about heaven. We know that heaven means the end of everything that we have found unpleasant or painful in life on earth. It means rest and peace after the toil and battle of earthly existence. It means positive joys which it is impossible to imagine now. Heaven means going home. Above all, it means the eternal vision of God.

Writing of the conditions which will prevail when the end of the world has come, St. John says: "He will wipe away every tear from their eyes, and there will be no more death, or mourning, or cries of distress, no more sorrow; those old things have passed away" (Apoc. 21:4). Many troubles and vexations mark our life in this world. It is a joy to know that heaven means the end of bodily ills, sickness, weariness, labor, poverty, worry, sorrow, regret, disappointment, doubt, fear, anxiety, temptation. Once heaven starts, we will never have to endure insincerity, dishonesty, envy or hatred.

There is further joy in the realization that heaven will

bring with it rest from all the labors and exertion of life on earth. It will bring peace after life's battle, light after its darkness.

After a hard day's work, we appreciate rest and relaxation. A feeling of restfulness bathes our whole being. In heaven all the effort and toil of life will be over, and an eternity of rest will lie before us.

We welcome the intervals of peace that interrupt the warfare of life in this world. When heaven begins for us, all struggle will be over forever. Eternal peace will stretch out before us.

We welcome the return of spring because springtide brings light after the darkness of winter, warmth after winter's coldness, the triumph of life over seeming death. Heaven is eternal springtide. When we enter heaven, we will leave behind the darkness and coldness of earthly life. Nature's resurgence in the springtime is only a weak reflection of the complete triumph over death which characterizes heaven.

Rest and peace may be looked on as negative advantages. Heaven will also bring positive joys so great that St. Paul, paraphrasing Isaias, referred to them in this way: "So we read of, Things no eye has seen, no ear has heard, no human heart conceived, the welcome God has prepared for those who love him" (I Cor. 2:9). While we have seen great beauty on earth, we will be grievously mistaken if we suppose that any beauty in this world can be compared with that of the world to come.

Our eyes have beheld the beauty of daybreak and sunset. We have often stood under a tree and have seen the already great beauty of the leaves enhanced by the light of the sun. We have been enthralled with the sight of undulating fields and rolling hills. We have had our breath taken away by a sudden view which made us feel that the world was at our feet. We are conscious of the charm of a rose, or of a human face. Our ears have had poured into them the ecstatic song of a bird, a masterpiece of music, a human voice of unearthly quality. And there is no limit to the beauty of which we may dream. Yet, none of these things can give us an idea of the beauty that awaits us in heaven.

There is joy in realizing that in heaven our bodies will be transformed. St. Paul, writing of the resurrection, says: "What is sown corruptible, rises incorruptible; what is sown unhonored, rises in glory; what is sown in weakness, is raised in power; what is sown a natural body, rises a spiritual body" (I Cor. 15:42-44). In heaven our glorified bodies obviously will be free from sickness and death. They will have a marvelous freedom of action. They will shine with a brightness reflected from our beatified souls.

The supreme joy that we anticipate, and the one that makes heaven what it is, is the vision of God. Only in the enjoyment of seeing God face to face can we experience that full expansion of our being, and that satisfaction of our vital powers, which we said were necessary for joy. We know even now that we were made for the one great purpose of being united with God, but we allow ourselves to be distracted from this truth. In heaven, the realization of it will strike us with blinding force. Then all happiness not enjoyed in God will appear to us hollow and unsatisfying.

We have all experienced times of great happiness on earth, but even at such times perhaps there was a feeling of uneasiness. Maybe in the back of our minds were such questions as, *How long will this last? When will the spell be broken?* The uneasiness is not hard to explain. Joy that has its roots in passing things must pass when they do. Joy that results from the possession of God must be eternal because he is eternal.

Part of our trouble is that since we have only a weak and hazy idea of God, our idea of heaven must be correspondingly weak. We get the impression that for many heaven means a place where they will enjoy to the *nth* degree all the pleasures they have experienced on earth. It takes a man like David to realize and express the truth that the essence of the joy of heaven is the vision of God. "With thy rich store thou wilt nourish them," says the psalmist, "bid them drink deep at thy fountain of contentment. In thee is the source of all life; thy brightness breaks on our eyes like dawn." (Ps. 35:9-10)

St. Paul warns against judging the joys of heaven by any experience we may have had on earth; by something, for example, that we may have seen: "This light and momentary affliction brings with it a reward multiplied every way, loading us with everlasting glory; if only we will fix our eyes on what is unseen, not on what we can see. What we can see, lasts but for a moment; what is unseen is eternal." (II Cor. 4:17-18) Here is the explanation for our eternal joy: we will see the unseen God.

When Moses spoke with God on Mount Sinai, the Lord told him: "My face thou canst not see; mortal man cannot see me, and live to tell of it." God, however, did allow Moses to see his glory in some reflected way: ". . . his face, although he did not know it, was all radiant after the meeting at which he had held speech with God." So great was the splendor that shone from the face of Moses that he had to veil it while speaking to the people. (Ex. 33:20, 34:29) We see here, by implication, how we will have to be transformed to see God face to face, as St. John tells us we will see him: "But we know that when he comes we shall be like him; we shall see him, then, as he is" (I Jn. 3:2).

In seeing God, we will see all things. In possessing him, we will possess all things. If you have admired some object of great beauty, it should bring you joy even now to realize that in heaven you will possess him of whom all other beauty and loveliness are only a pale reflection. If you have yearned to acquire knowledge of some tantalizing or mysterious subject, it should be a source of joy to you even on earth to be assured that in heaven you will be filled with the knowledge of all things that God has created, and with the knowledge of God himself.

If you have enjoyed the companionship of human beings of great intellectual depth, personal charm and estimable character, it should bring you great satisfaction to know that in heaven you will be inebriated with the vision and presence of him in whom all that is deep, attractive and worthy in human beings has its source. If you have loved somebody with a great, enduring and holy love, you should rejoice that in possessing God in heaven, you will also possess this loved one with all his or her lovable qualities purified, heightened and divinized.

Magnanimous men often give far more than is due in justice to others, and in acting thus they are imitating the lavishness of God in pouring out his rewards. In considering heaven, we have only to remember that we are dealing with the God of infinite power and munificence.